CONTEMPORARY'S

CHOICES
AN ESL LIFESKILLS SERIES FOR ADULTS
FAMILIES AND SCHOOLS

RIDGEWATER COLLEGE
Hutchinson Campus
2 Century Ave SE
Hutchinson MN 55350-3183

CHOICES
AN ESL LIFESKILLS SERIES FOR ADULTS
FAMILIES AND SCHOOLS

JANE YEDLIN
WITH
CAROLINE T. LINSE

Project Editor
Marietta Urban

Consultants
Ann Van Slyke
ESL Consultant
Atlanta, Georgia

Terence J. Bray
Hacienda La Puente
Unified School District
Hacienda Heights, California

CONTEMPORARY
BOOKS
CHICAGO

Library of Congress Catalog-in-Publication Data

Yedlin, Jane.
   Families and schools / Jane Yedlin.
      p.   cm—(Choices : an ESL lifeskills series)
   Includes index.
   ISBN 0-8092-4046-7 (paper)
      1. English language—Textbooks for foreign
speakers.   2. Readers—Schools.   3. Readers—
Family.   4. Life skills.   I. Title   II. Series: Choices
(Chicago, Ill.)
PE1128.Y44   1991
428.6'4—dc20   9'-15259
                                                                     CIP

This book is dedicated to George, Max, and Jesse, with
love and thanks for the gift of time.

Choices: An ESL Lifeskills Series for Adults was developed
for Contemporary Books by **Quest Editorial Development,
Inc.**

Published by Contemporary Books, Inc.
180 North Michigan Avenue, Chicago, Illinois 60601
Manufactured in the United States of America
International Standard Book Number: 0-8092-

Published simultaneously in Canada by
Fitzhenry & Whiteside
91 Granton Drive
Richmond Hill, Ontario L4B 2N5
Canada

Consultants
Ann Van Slyke
Terence J. Bray

Editorial Director
Caren Van Slyke

Senior Editor
Julie Landau

Editorial
Lisa Black
Laura Larson
Jane Samuelson
Charlotte Ullman
Cliff Wirt

Editorial Production Manager
Norma Fioretti

Production Editor
Jean Farley Brown

Production Assistant
Marina Micari

Cover Design
Georgene Sainati

Illustrator
Gary Undercuffler

Cover photograph © C. C. Cain

■■■■■ Contents

■ ■ ■ ■ ■ To the Student

Welcome to *Families and Schools*!

Families and Schools is part of Contemporary's *Choices: An ESL Lifeskills Series for Adults.*

The purpose of this book is to give you information about family and education issues in the United States. *Families and Schools* will also give you the language skills you need to use that information.

You already know about family concerns in your native country. *Families and Schools* encourages you to compare the way you do things in your native country with the way you do things in the United States.

Families and Schools offers valuable information about:

- prenatal care
- choosing daycare
- registering children for school
- understanding report cards
- child safety products
- after-school programs for children
- parental involvement in their children's schools
- continuing education for adults

and many other family choices in the United States.

We hope you enjoy *Families and Schools* and that it will help you in making choices for you and your family.

Level

Choices: An ESL Lifeskills Series for Adults is designed for ESL students who are at the intermediate level. **Choices** will guide students in making informed decisions about their lives in the U.S., based on the knowledge they bring from their native countries. **Choices** will help students acquire the lifeskills competencies, language skills, and cultural information they need to make effective choices in the U.S.

Rationale

Families and Schools provides a student-centered approach to language learning. It offers detailed information about family and education issues in the U.S. while providing opportunities for cultural comparison and teaching practical language skills. The **Choices** series features natural language that adult students can put to immediate use in their daily lives.

Format

Families and Schools contains a *Tips for Teachers* section, twelve chapters, four review units, an appendix, and an index. The review units are interactive information-gap exercises that appear after every three chapters, incorporating content from those chapters. The authors acknowledge Judy Winn-Bell Olsen and Richard C. Yorkey as sources of inspiration for these exercises.

> For step-by-step information on how to use this book and for additional classroom activities, see **Choices Teacher's Guide 1**.

Tips for Teachers

Everyone from the beginning teacher to the experienced professional can benefit from teaching suggestions. What follows are notes on the purpose of the sections in *Families and Schools* and how to use them.

The **Before You Listen** section prepares students for the dialogue by encouraging them to discuss the picture that illustrates it. Ask students to predict what they think will happen in the dialogue. This is a good time for you to assess how much the students know about the topic. If you want to teach key words before students listen to the dialogue, consult the **Words to Know** section.

There are a number of ways to present the **Dialogue**. It is helpful to act out the dialogue, doing something to indicate that you are portraying different people talking. For example, you may want to use different voices or change positions as you change roles. If the resources are available, you may wish to record the dialogue ahead of time. If you do this, make sure each character is vocally distinct, so that students know who is talking.

Discuss the dialogue, using the **Talking It Over** questions as a guide. Ask students if they have had experiences similar to the situation in the dialogue.

Assign different groups of students to different roles corresponding to characters in the dialogue. Have them repeat their roles after you. Have students practice the dialogue in pairs or groups. Ask for volunteers to perform the dialogue for the class. Most of the dialogues are open ended. Have students invent their own endings.

Words to Know presents vocabulary that students need to know in order to understand the dialogue. The blank lines allow students to personalize the text by adding their own words to the vocabulary list. Encourage students to guess the meaning of vocabulary through the context and to refer back to the picture.

Another Way to Say It offers alternatives for some of the idiomatic expressions that are introduced in the dialogue. Have students read the dialogue again, inserting the new expressions. The blank lines in this section allow students to personalize the text by adding their own words to the vocabulary list.

Talking It Over should foster discussion about the situation presented in the dialogue and invite students to talk about how their own experiences relate to the situation. The questions in this section range from simple comprehension to application of the information to students' lives.

In **Working Together**, a role-play activity, students create conversations and put to use the language they have just learned. You may want to write the sample conversation on the board and ask students what they think should come next. Write their ideas on the board. After students have written the conversation as a class, have them practice it in pairs or groups and ask for volunteers to role-play it for the class. Then, have students create individual conversations based on relevant experiences.

Real Talk shows students how speakers of American English really talk. For that reason, it's important to pronounce naturally when you present this section.

Putting It Together presents grammar in context. It focuses on one useful structure that appears in the dialogue. There is a short presentation of the structure and then a contextual exercise. This is followed by the opportunity to use the structure in meaningful, real-life responses.

In the **Read and Think** sections, students are asked to guess the meanings of underlined words. The content reading on this page provides information that students can put to use immediately. The **Read and Think** page is a reading passage or an example of the kinds of reading materials that people have to deal with every day, such as leases, warranties, phone bills, bank statements, and school and medical forms.

In Your Community offers students an opportunity to explore the community resources available to them. They can do this individually or in pairs or groups. You may also want to take students to a community-based organization during class time, invite a speaker to the classroom, or bring in realia such as the classified section of the newspaper.

Figuring Out the U.S. features an intimate look at one aspect of U.S. culture. Students are encouraged to circle any words in the passage they don't understand and to try to guess their meanings from the context.

Your Turn gives the students the chance to compare life here with life in their native countries and opens up avenues to a variety of choices. Depending on the proficiency level of your students, the writing activity may range from a simple list to a paragraph or more expressing an opinion.

1 Don't Worry

Before You Listen

1. Where are these people?
2. Why are the women there?
3. Why is the man there?
4. What do you think they are talking about?

■■■■■ Don't Worry

Listen carefully to the dialogue.

Mrs. Santos:	Hello. I saw you here last month.
Mrs. Chem:	Yes. I remember. I'll be here next week, but I hope we won't meet here again next month.
Mrs. Santos:	What do you mean? Oh, is your baby due soon?
Mrs. Chem:	Yes, I'm due in about ten days. I can't wait.
Mrs. Santos:	I can wait. I'm so scared. I want my mother with me.
Mrs. Chem:	I think we're all scared the first time. You'll be fine. Don't worry.
Mrs. Santos:	I'm afraid here. In my village, we don't have babies in hospitals. Women have babies at home.
Mr. Williams:	Excuse me, but the doctors are very good here. My wife is forty years old, and we just had our first baby . . .
Mrs. Chem:	Forty years old?
Mr. Williams:	Yes. She's in now for her six-week checkup. She was scared too, but her pregnancy and delivery went smoothly.
Mrs. Santos:	But who will help me with my baby? I won't know what to do. I want to have my baby in my country!
Mrs. Chem:	Well, in my country there is war and not enough to eat. Many babies get sick and die. I feel lucky to have my babies here.

Words to Know

I'm due	scared	pregnancy
can't wait	checkup	delivery
_____	_____	_____

Another Way to Say It

Don't worry. .... Take it easy.
went smoothly .... was fine/went OK

_____ .... _____

■ ■ ■ ■ ■ Talking It Over

Discuss the questions in pairs or groups.

1. Mrs. Santos does not want to have her baby in the U.S. Look at the dialogue again, and find her reasons.
2. Do you think she has other reasons? What might they be?
3. Mrs. Chem feels lucky to have her babies in the United States. Make a list of some good things about having children in the U.S.
4. Mrs. Chem and Mrs. Santos both feel fine. Why are they in the clinic? How often do they go there?
5. Mr. Williams's wife already had her baby, and everything went smoothly. Why are they at the clinic?
6. When Mr. and Mrs. Williams leave the Obstetric Clinic, they will go to the Pediatric Clinic. Why will they go there?
7. What did Mr. Williams say about his wife that surprised Mrs. Chem? Does it surprise you?
8. In the United States, many women have first babies when they are over thirty years old. Does this happen in your native country very often? Why do you think it happens in the U.S.? What are some advantages and disadvantages of having children at an older age?

Working Together

Work with your classmates and teacher to finish this conversation. Then practice with a partner.

Imagine you are a friend of Mrs. Santos. You want her to feel better. What can you say to her?

Mrs. Santos: I'm so scared!
    Friend: Don't worry. Everything will be fine.

Real Talk

English speakers pronounce -*tion* and -*cian* like "shun." Listen to your teacher say these words:

congratulations   obstetrician
examination   pediatrician
invitation   physician
tradition

> ### Will/Won't
>
> Use *will* to talk about the future. *Will* can be shortened (contracted) to *'ll*:
>
> | | |
> |---|---|
> | I **will** -> I'll | we **will** -> we'll |
> | you **will** -> you'll | you **will** -> you'll |
> | he **will** -> he'll | they **will** -> they'll |
> | she **will** -> she'll | |
> | it **will** -> it'll | |
>
>   **I'll** be here again next week.
>
> The negative form is *will not*. The contracted form is *won't*.
>   I **won't** know what to do.

Practice A

Listen as your teacher reads the dialogue. Listen for sentences containing a form of *will* or *won't*. Write the sentence(s) on the lines below. Then read the dialogue to check your answer.

_____

_____

Express hopes for the future with *hope + will* or *won't*.

Practice B

Write two sentences about your hopes for yourself and for your family. Use *will* and *won't*. Discuss your answers in small groups.

_____

_____

Read the passage and try to guess the meanings of the underlined words. Rephrase each paragraph. Then answer the questions.

Prenatal Care

It is very important for a woman to have a medical checkup as soon as she knows she is <u>pregnant</u>. <u>Prenatal</u> care can prevent many <u>birth defects</u>, such as some <u>deformities</u> or <u>low birth weight</u>. Prenatal care includes going to the doctor, eating well, and avoiding <u>dangerous substances</u>.

During the first visit to the <u>obstetrician</u>, a pregnant woman has an <u>examination</u>, a weight check, and some blood tests. Then she returns to the doctor once a month. During the last month, she goes once a week.

Another important part of prenatal care is eating well. Meals should include a variety of foods. <u>Vitamins and minerals</u>, especially calcium and iron, are a necessary part of a pregnant woman's <u>diet</u>.

Prenatal care also includes avoiding dangerous substances. Smoking, drinking <u>alcoholic beverages</u> such as beer and wine, and taking drugs can harm the unborn baby. Even <u>nonprescription drugs</u>, such as aspirin and cough medicine, can be dangerous.

During her <u>pregnancy</u>, a woman needs to decide if she will <u>breast-feed</u> her baby. In the recent past, the most popular way to feed an infant was from a bottle. Nowadays, many American women prefer to breast-feed their babies. Experts claim that the mother's milk is healthier than baby <u>formula</u>.

1. What is prenatal care?
2. What three things can hurt the unborn baby?

In Your Community

Find out the information individually or in groups, and share it with your class.

1. Where do women in your community go for prenatal care and to have babies?
2. Where do families in your community take their babies for well-baby care and immunizations?
3. Is free or low-cost care available in these places?
4. Find out if these places have medical workers or translators who speak your native language. Do you need to make arrangements in advance for translators?
5. If you work, find out what kinds of maternity leave, job security, or benefits your employer provides.

■ ■ ■ ■ ■ ■ Figuring Out the U.S.

As you read the passage, circle the words you don't understand and try to guess their meanings.

Customs

1. **Many women who work stay at their jobs until a short time before their babies are due.** If their jobs are very difficult physically, they may need to stop sooner.

2. **Pregnant women do not "hide" at home.** They work, go shopping, take walks, go out at night, exercise, and go to the beach. They are seen everywhere.

3. **Many women go to classes to prepare for the birth of a baby.** The women and their partners learn all about labor and delivery. In the classes, the women practice special ways to breathe and to relax that will help make the delivery easier.

4. **What is a baby shower?** It is the name of a party that friends and relatives give for mothers-to-be. At the baby shower, the guests bring presents for the baby, such as clothes, toys, and equipment.

5. **Why do baby shower invitations sometimes have a bird on them?** The bird is a stork, and it is a symbol of childbirth. It is used because in folktales storks deliver babies to houses.

6. **Why are so many baby things pink and blue?** Pink is the traditional color for a girl, and blue is the traditional color for a boy.

7. **What is the man in the picture giving to his friends?** Cigars used to be a traditional gift from a new father to his friends.

Your Turn

Discuss the questions.

1. Do pregnant women in your native country continue their normal activities until the baby is born?
2. How do families prepare for the birth of a baby in your native country?
3. What folktales explain how babies are born?
4. Are there special customs to celebrate the birth of a baby?
5. Imagine you or your partner is having a baby. What traditions of your native country would you keep? What U.S. customs would you adopt?

> *Choose one of the questions and write about it.*

2 And Baby Makes Three

Before You Listen

1. Who are the people in this picture? What is their relationship?
2. How do you think they feel?
3. What do you think they are talking about?
4. Why do you think the baby is crying?

■■■■■ And Baby Makes Three

Listen carefully to the dialogue.

Mrs. Williams: I went to the school office today. I told the principal that I'll return to work in three months.

Mr. Williams: Return to work? What are you talking about?

Mrs. Williams: I told you that I was thinking about going back. I miss teaching.

Mr. Williams: Your most important job right now is being a mother. Who will take care of the baby all day long?

Mrs. Williams: Crystal will be a year old in three months. I've already visited a few daycare centers. Some of them look very good.

Mr. Williams: I won't put my daughter in any daycare center! I make enough money to support us. You should be happy to stay home and take care of your OWN child!

Mrs. Williams: But I love my job, and I'm good at it. It makes me feel good.

Mr. Williams: Haven't you heard what happens to children at daycare centers? A child should be at home with her mother.

Mrs. Williams: It will be good for her to be around other children her age.

Words to Know

principal	daycare center	own
miss	enough	_____
take care of	support	_____
_____	_____	_____

Another Way to Say It

return to work .... go back to work
stay home .... be a full-time housewife
be around .... have contact with
_____ .... _____
_____ .... _____

■ ■ ■ ■ ■ Talking It Over

Discuss the questions in pairs or groups.

1. Mrs. Williams did something that surprised her husband. What was it?
2. Mr. Williams doesn't want his wife to work. He wants her to stay home. Look at the dialogue again, and find his reasons. List all of the reasons he gives in the dialogue.
3. Do you think he has other reasons? What might they be?
4. Mrs. Williams wants to go back to work. Look at the dialogue again, and find her reasons. List all of the reasons she gives in the dialogue.
5. Do you think that she has other reasons? What might they be?
6. What did Mrs. Williams do to make sure that she found a good daycare center for her child?
7. Mr. Williams is concerned that bad things might happen to their daughter in the daycare center. What bad things could happen?
8. Mrs. Williams feels that it will be good for her daughter to be in daycare. How do children benefit by being in daycare?

Working Together

Work with your classmates and teacher to finish this conversation. Then practice with a partner.

    Wife: I want to go back to work now that the baby is nine months old.
Husband: No. I don't want you to.
    Wife: Why not?

Real Talk

Americans express surprise by repeating as a question all or part of what was just said. Listen to Mr. Williams's reaction:

    Mrs. Williams: *I'll return to work in three months.*
    Mr. Williams: *Return to work?*

The voice rises at the end of the sentence to show surprise.

■ ■ ■ ■ ■ ■ Putting It Together

> **Comparatives**
>
> clean   clean**er**
> happy   happ**ier**
> attractive   **more** attractive
>
> Kiddy Korner is clean**er** than the Child Development Center.

Mr. and Mrs. Williams are looking for a good daycare center for their daughter. Today they visited two daycare centers: *Kiddy Korner* and the *Child Development Center*. Mr. Williams prefers *Kiddy Korner*. Mrs. Williams likes the *Child Development Center*. They are arguing about which center is better. Compare the two daycare centers as in number 1.

1. **Mrs. Williams:** The Child Development Center is very attractive.
   Mr. Williams: Kiddy Korner is more attractive.

2. **Mr. Williams:** Kiddy Korner is very convenient.
   Mrs. Williams: _____

3. **Mrs. Williams:** The toys at the Child Development Center are very educational.
   Mr. Williams: _____

4. **Mrs. Williams:** The Child Development Center is very clean.
   Mr. Williams: _____

5. **Mr. Williams:** The playground at Kiddy Korner is very large.
   Mrs. Williams: _____

6. **Mr. Williams:** The bathroom at the Child Development Center was dirty!
   Mrs. Williams: _____

7. **Mrs. Williams:** The children at the Child Development Center seem very happy.
   Mr. Williams: _____

■■■■■ Read and Think

Read the passage and try to guess the meanings of the underlined words.
Rephrase each paragraph. Then answer the questions.

Kinds of Daycare

There are two main types of daycare: <u>family</u> <u>home</u> <u>daycare</u> and <u>institutional</u> <u>daycare</u>. The family home daycare <u>provider</u> takes care of a child or a small group of children in her own home. Institutional daycare includes: daycare centers, headstart <u>programs</u>, nursery schools, and preschools. They may have buildings of their own, or they may be <u>located</u> in churches, temples, hospitals, community buildings, or <u>work</u> <u>sites</u>.

Why do some families prefer home daycare?

The hours are more flexible. If I have to work late, my son can eat dinner there.—the mother of a four-year-old boy

It's a family's home. It's warm and cozy. My daughter is too little for a school.—the mother of a one-year-old girl

Why do some families prefer institutional daycare?

There are several staff members, not just one. I don't have to worry if the provider or her family gets sick.—the father of three-year-old twins

1. What are the main differences between family home daycare and institutional daycare?
2. Which would you prefer?

In Your Community

Work in small groups to find out about child care in your community. Use resources you may know and others suggested in the Appendix. Fill in the chart below.

Draw your own group chart and fill in the following information:

	Provider A	Provider B	Provider C
Name of provider			
Telephone number			
Ages of children			
Hours			
Cost per week			
Are meals provided?			

■■■■■ Figuring Out the U.S.

As you read the passage, circle the words you don't understand and try to guess their meanings.

Choosing Daycare

In the United States today, many couples live far away from their families. With no grandmothers, aunts, or other relatives nearby, working parents must find other people to care for their children.

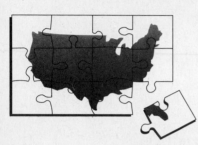

Child care is a big problem for working parents in the U.S. It is often difficult to find a safe, inexpensive place that cares for young children.

It is important to visit daycare providers before you decide which will be the best for your child. When you visit one, make the most of your visit. Look around and ask questions.

What to look for:

–Is the building clean and cheerful?

–Do the children look happy and well cared for?

–Is there a schedule of activities?

–Are the children playing, or are they watching TV?

–Does the provider read to the children?

–How is food prepared and served?

–How does the provider discipline children and keep order?

–How does the care provider treat the children?

–Do you see safety problems, such as damaged electrical cords, unprotected heaters or radiators, or sharp objects?

What to ask:

–Do you have a license?

–Do you have references?

–Are children allowed to come when they are sick?

–How many adults take care of how many children?

–Can parents visit anytime to observe?

Your Turn

Discuss the questions.

1. Who takes care of the children of working parents in your native country? Do grandparents and aunts help out?
2. Does the government provide daycare?
3. What are some important things to look for when selecting daycare?
4. What are some advantages and disadvantages of daycare for children?

> *Choose one of the questions and write about it.*

3 You're Late!

Before You Listen

1. Who are the people in this picture?
2. What is their relationship?
3. What are they doing?
4. Why do you think the mother is angry?
5. How do you think the daughter feels?

▪▪▪▪▪ You're Late!

Listen carefully to the dialogue.

Mrs. Diaz: You're late!

Corazon: It's only 5 o'clock.

Mrs. Diaz: You're supposed to be here at 3:15. Where were you?

Corazon: I was at school at a play rehearsal. Mrs. Reynolds, my English teacher, asked me to help paint scenery.

Mrs. Diaz: Scenery?

Corazon: Yes. I painted mountains and trees with some other kids. I talked with them in English. Mrs. Reynolds said it was good practice for me.

Mrs. Diaz: I don't care what your teacher said. You're supposed to come home right after school. I was worried about you!

Corazon: Oh, Mama, there's nothing to worry about.

Mrs. Diaz: There are many things for mothers to worry about when they are raising children alone. Oh no, it's already 5:15. I'm late for work! I'm supposed to BE there at 5:15 on Thursdays.

Corazon: I'm sorry I forgot.

Mrs. Diaz: Feed your brothers, and don't forget to give them a bath before you put them to bed. Do your homework. No TV . . .

Corazon: But, Mama . . .

Mrs. Diaz: And no talking on the telephone until all hours. Be in bed by 10.

Words to Know

play	scenery	already
rehearsal	practice	late for
_____	_____	_____

Another Way to Say It

you're supposed to .... you should
I don't care .... it's not important
there's nothing to worry about .... everything is all right
until all hours .... until very late
_____ .... _____

■■■■■ Talking It Over

Discuss the questions in pairs or groups.

1. Why is Mrs. Diaz so angry at her daughter? Why was she worried?
2. Where was her daughter? What was she doing?
3. What time was she supposed to be home?
4. Why did the English teacher think it was a good idea for Corazon to stay after school?
5. What responsibilities does Corazon have at home?
6. What responsibilities does Mrs. Diaz have?
7. How do single working mothers meet all of their responsibilities?
8. How does Corazon feel?
9. How does Mrs. Diaz feel?
10. Do parents have problems like this in your native country?

Working Together

Work with your classmates and teacher to finish this conversation. Then practice with a partner.

Mrs. Reynolds calls Mrs. Diaz on the telephone to ask if Corazon can stay after school every day to paint.

Mrs. Reynolds: Can Corazon stay after school every day to paint scenery?

Mrs. Diaz: No! She's supposed to come home right away.

Real Talk

People sometimes pronounce *supposed to* so it sounds like "spose ta." You do not need to pronounce it this way, and you should never write it this way. But knowing this will help you understand when people pronounce it this way. Listen to your teacher say this sentence.

You're *supposed to* do your homework.

Supposed to

Use a form of *be + supposed to* to talk about following rules or doing what other people expect someone to do.

I am		be here.
You/We/They are	**supposed to**	come home.
He/She/It is		_____.

Use *not supposed to* to express negative rules.

Corazon is **not supposed to** talk on the telephone until all hours.

Practice A

What does Mrs. Diaz expect Corazon to do tonight? Write sentences with *supposed to*.

1. _____
2. _____
3. _____
4. _____

Practice B

What doesn't Mrs. Diaz want Corazon to do tonight? Write sentences with *not supposed to*.

1. _____
2. _____
3. _____

Practice C

What rules do you expect **your** children to follow? Write two sentences with *supposed to* and two sentences with *not supposed to*. Share your answers with the class.

1. _____
2. _____
3. _____
4. _____

■■■■■ Read and Think

Read the passage and try to guess the meanings of the underlined words.
Rephrase each paragraph. Then answer the questions.

Disciplining Children

Not all parents agree about how to discipline children. Experts generally agree, however, that children who <u>misbehave</u> need to stop and think about what they did wrong. Then they can learn from the experience. All child specialists agree that striking a child is a harmful way to discipline a child.

Younger children sometimes need <u>time out</u> after they do something wrong, such as hitting another child. They are told to stop and sit alone in a quiet place for a short time. This gives the child a chance to "cool down" and think about the <u>naughty behavior</u>. The child stays there for five to fifteen minutes.

Older children may be <u>grounded</u> when they misbehave. This means they can leave the house only to go to school or work or for necessary activities. This form of discipline gives the older child enough time to think about his or her behavior. A child may be grounded for a day, a week, or a month.

Another way to discipline an older child is to take away his or her <u>privileges</u>. Privileges, such as dessert, television, computer games, and parties, may be taken away from the child for an hour, a day, a week, or even a month. This helps teach children that they must behave well in order to get things or do things that they enjoy.

1. What do all three forms of discipline have in common?
2. In what ways are the first two different from the third?
3. Do you ever have to discipline your children? How do they feel about it? How do you feel?

In Your Community

Interview class members who are parents, your friends or relatives who have children, and your teacher. Ask these questions:

1. At what age should a parent start disciplining a child?
2. How would you discipline a two-year-old who bites a playmate?
3. How would you discipline a seven-year-old who hits another seven-year-old?
4. How would you discipline an eight-year-old who has hit a five-year-old?
5. How would you discipline a fifteen-year-old boy who stayed out all night?

In a small group, make a chart comparing the answers you receive.

■ ■ ■ ■ ■ Figuring Out the U.S.

As you read the script from a TV talk show, circle the words you don't understand and try to guess their meanings.

Changes in Family Life

Host: I have with me today several people who have come to the U.S. recently. We're going to talk about how living in the U.S. has changed their family life. Jerun, would you begin?

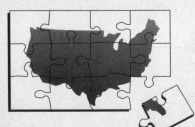

Jerun: Yes. I am from Thailand, and in my country I was a housewife and had a maid to help me. In this country, I do two jobs. I work in a factory, and I do all of the housework. My husband works outside the home too. We need two salaries just to make ends meet. My children are home alone after school.

Pedro: I'm from Mexico. My wife doesn't listen anymore since we came to the United States. She earns as much money as I do. When I tell her to do something, now she argues with me.

Lupe: In our village in Bolivia, there were not many bad things for children to do. There were no gangs or drugs. Of course, sometimes your child did something like steal or get too friendly with the opposite sex. If that happened, you heard about it right away. Someone was always watching: relatives, godparents, or neighbors. Once the priest caught my daughter holding hands with a boy. But here . . .

Stanislav: I'm from Poland, and my biggest problem is the language. I can't speak English very well, and I have to take my daughter with me to translate. I feel embarrassed when we can't pay our bills and I have to send a ten-year-old girl to explain. It makes her feel worried too.

Your Turn

1. Divide into four groups. Each group will make a list of solutions for one speaker's problems. When the lists are finished, each group should share their solutions with the class. Other classmates may then make comments and suggestions.
2. In addition to the problems described above, what other problems do families face when they come to the U.S.? What can people do about these problems?

> *Choose one of the problems families face and write about it.*

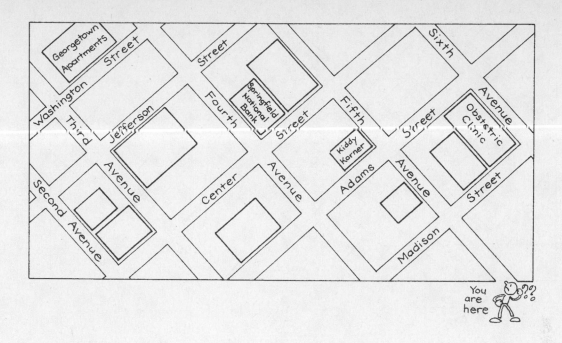

Person A

You need directions to **Jefferson School, the Child Development Center, General Hospital**, and **Springfield High School**. Your map shows these buildings but does not show their names. Your partner's map does show the names. Ask your partner for directions to these places. Use words. Do not point. Do not look at each other's maps until you are finished.

Your partner will ask you later for directions to places that are named on your map.

When you finish, there will still be some buildings with no names. Work together to decide what these places are. Write the names on the buildings. Draw another person somewhere on your map, and write directions to get your person to the buildings you have just labeled.

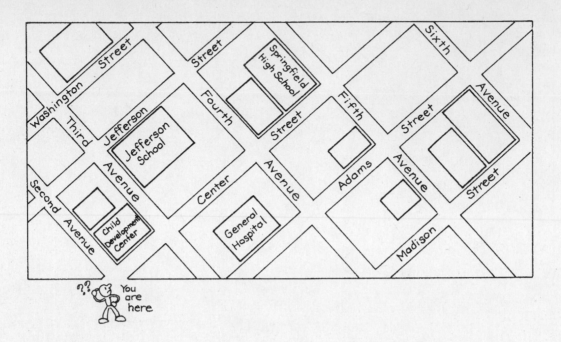

Person B

You need directions to **Georgetown Apartments**, **Kiddy Korner**, **Springfield National Bank**, and the **Obstetric Clinic**. Your map shows these buildings but does not show their names. Your partner's map does show the names. Ask your partner for directions to these places. Use words. Do not point. Do not look at each other's maps until you are finished.

Your partner will ask you for directions to places that are named on your map.

When you finish, there will still be some buildings with no names. Work together to decide what these places are. Write the names on the buildings. Draw another person somewhere on your map, and write directions to get your person to the buildings you have just labeled.

Before You Listen

1. Where are these people?
2. Who are the people in this picture? What is their relationship?
3. What is Mr. Williams's job?
4. What is Bernardo's job?
5. What do you think they are talking about?

■■■■■ I Might Quit School

Listen carefully to the dialogue.

Mr. Williams: Bernardo, I need a daytime janitor too. Do you have any friends who can work full time?

Bernardo: I can, Mr. Williams. I might quit school anyway. My family needs more money.

Mr. Williams: You can't drop out. You're too young.

Bernardo: No, I'm not. I was sixteen last week.

Mr. Williams: Sixteen or not, it would be a big mistake. This is a dead-end job. Stay in school and graduate.

Bernardo: I'm not a very good student. Besides, what can I do with a high school diploma?

Mr. Williams: Bernardo, you're a smart guy. If you get a high school diploma, I can get you into a training program here at the bank. You can work here full time and earn your college degree at night.

Bernardo: But I don't need college. I need money.

Mr. Williams: You'll make more money in the long run if you have an education. You'll help your family more. They'll be proud.

Bernardo: My parents need help now! They're both old. They work day and night just to make ends meet. You don't know what it's like for us.

Mr. Williams: Yes, I do.

Words to Know

janitor	besides	degree
mistake	diploma	proud
graduate	guy	_____

Another Way to Say It

quit school	drop out of school
dead-end job	job with no future
in the long run	in the future
make ends meet	have enough money to live

■■■■■ Talking It Over

Discuss the questions in pairs or groups.

1. Why does Mr. Williams need another janitor? Is Bernardo doing a good job? Why do you think so?
2. Why does Bernardo want to drop out of school?
3. Why does Mr. Williams think Bernardo should stay in school?
4. What do you think Bernardo should do? Why?
5. How do you think Bernardo's parents will feel if Bernardo quits school?
6. What could Bernardo do to get better grades in school?
7. Teenagers are allowed to leave school when they turn sixteen years old in most states in the U.S. How long do students have to stay in school in your native country? Is it the same for boys and girls?
8. What jobs do you think Bernardo can get if he finishes school and attends the job training program?

Working Together

Work with your classmates and teacher to finish this conversation. Then practice with a partner.

> **Bernardo:** I'm thinking about dropping out of school.
> **Mr. Williams:** That would be a big mistake.

Real Talk

Sometimes it is difficult to hear the difference between *can* and *can't* in a sentence. Listen to your teacher say these sentences:

I *can* work.
I *can't* work.

The verb after *can* is stressed in most affirmative sentences. *Can't* is stressed in most negative sentences.

Work with a partner. Make up your own sentences using *can* or *can't*. See if your partner understands you.

> **If. . ., can/can't**
>
> Use *can/can't* to express ability or permission.
>
> Examples: If Bernardo graduates, he **can** begin a training program at the bank.
>
> If Bernardo quits school, he **can't** get a better job.

Practice A

Make sentences about what Bernardo can or can't do.

1. If Bernardo stays in school, he can _____.
2. If Bernardo needs help in school, he can_____.
3. If Bernardo goes to college at night, _____.
4. If Bernardo quits school, he can't _____.
5. If Bernardo is sick, he can't _____.

Practice B

Write sentences about yourself and your family. Share them with the class.

1. If I _____.
2. If I _____.
3. If my _____.
4. If my _____.

■■■■■ Read and Think

Read the help wanted ads carefully. Then fill in the chart with the information from the ads. If the information is not given, put a question mark (?) in the space.

Job Guide

Data Entry Clerk
Must be able to work under pressure. Opportunity for advancement and future training. Send resume to: Box 8083.

Janitor
Needed for bank to open soon. No experience required. Hourly pay. Apply in person M-F, 10-4 5120 Adams Street.

Legal Secretary
Salary to $24,000. Previous experience or training as a legal secretary required. H.S. diploma and secretarial school certificate required. Typing 65 wpm, shorthand, and word-processing skills required. Call Linda for appt. 555-1530.

Retail Salespersons
Salary depends on exper. H.S. diploma required. Oppty. for advancement. Excellent benefits. Non-smoking. Call Personnel for interview: 555-7504.

Shoe Repair Person
Experience preferred but will train enthusiastic, responsible person. Starting salary $4/hr. and benefits. H.S. diploma required. Annual raises. Call 555-0580.

Translators
Spanish and Cantonese. Translate publications from English to language. Type 45 wpm. Prefer native speakers. Call 555-0300.

Job	Experience or training	Education	Advancement	Salary/ Benefits
Shoe Repair	Preferred	H.S. diploma	annual raises	$4 an hr/yes

In Your Community

What job or field are you interested in? Form groups according to your interests. Work with your group to find out about that job or field from your local newspaper. Then make a group chart like the one above and post it in your classroom.

■■■■■ Figuring Out the U.S.

As you read the passage, circle the words you don't understand and try to guess their meanings.

I Have a Dream

I have a dream that my four little children will one day live in a
nation where they will not be judged by the color of their skin,
but [by] the content of their character.
I have a dream today!
I have a dream that one day . . . little black boys and black girls
will be able to join hands with little white boys and white girls
as sisters and brothers.
I have a dream today!

Martin Luther King, Jr., 1963

In the U.S., education is seen as a ladder that helps people to move up.
People with an education get better jobs and earn more money. The

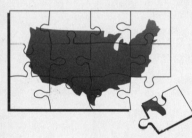

dream of most Americans is a good education for their
children so that their children's lives will be happier and
easier.

There are laws in the U.S. that promise equal
educational opportunities for children of all colors, all
nationalities, and all languages. In the U.S., you do not
have to be rich to get a good education.

People like Martin Luther King, Jr., fought for these laws. Dr. King and
other civil rights leaders saw that poor black children were not receiving a
good education. Their schools were separate and inferior. The leaders
protested these conditions, and some changes were made. Today, in many
U.S. cities, parents still think that their children are not receiving an equal
education. The struggle for racial equality continues.

Your Turn

Discuss the questions.

1. What dreams do you have for your children?
2. The U.S. has been called "the land of opportunity." What does that mean?
3. What opportunities did you expect to find here?
4. What opportunities are not available?
5. Thomas Edison said, "Education makes the man [woman]." What did
   he mean by this? Is this true today in the United States? Is this true in
   your native country?

> *Choose one of the questions and write about it.*

5 How Old Is Mei?

Before You Listen

1. Where are these people?
2. Why do you think they are there?
3. What will the secretary ask?

■■■■■ How Old Is Mei?

Listen carefully to the dialogue.

Mrs. Tuy: Excuse me. I would like to register my daughter Mei for school.

Mrs. Feingold: Yes, ma'am. Do you have a birth certificate, passport, or baptismal certificate for her?

Mrs. Tuy: Yes, right here. What else do I need?

Mrs. Feingold: You need immunization records and proof of address. Where do you live?

Mrs. Tuy: I live just around the corner at 96 Third Avenue. We are living with my sister, Mrs. Chem.

Mrs. Feingold: Do you have a driver's license for proof of address?

Mrs. Tuy: Certainly. Here's my license.

Mrs. Feingold: You live in this school district. I'm not sure if Mei should go to this elementary school or to the junior high school.

Mrs. Tuy: Oh, I want her to go to this school.

Mrs. Feingold: What grades has she completed?

Mrs. Tuy: I don't know. They gave lots of English classes in the refugee camp. She's twelve.

Mrs. Feingold: Well, I think she should go to the junior high school.

Mrs. Tuy: Can't she go to school here with her sister and cousins?

Mrs. Feingold: No, but the bus will take her to the junior high school.

Words to Know

ma'am	immunization records	grades
birth certificate	driver's license	refugee camp
baptismal certificate	school district	cousins
passport	elementary	_____

Another Way to Say It

excuse me .... pardon me
register for school .... enroll in school
just around the corner .... nearby, very close
certainly .... of course, sure
completed .... finished

Talking It Over

Discuss the questions in pairs or groups.

1. Mrs. Tuy wants her daughter, Mei, to go to the neighborhood elementary school. Look at the dialogue and find her reasons.
2. Mrs. Feingold thinks that Mei should go to junior high school. Look at the dialogue again, and find her reasons.
3. Why do you think Mrs. Tuy needs immunization records and proof of address to register Mei for school? Why does she also need a birth certificate, passport, or baptismal certificate for her daughter?
4. Why does Mrs. Feingold want to know what grades Mei has completed? How can the school find out what grade Mei belongs in?
5. What do you think? Should Mei go to the neighborhood elementary school or to the junior high school? Why?
6. Mrs. Feingold is the school secretary. She helps parents register their children for school. How else do school secretaries help parents and students?

Working Together

Work with a partner to finish this conversation. You want to talk to your child's teacher. You call your school secretary to leave a message for your child's teacher to return your call.

Mrs. Feingold:	Hello. Jefferson Elementary School. May I help you?
You:	This is Mrs. (Mr.) _____ speaking. I would like to talk to _____ about my son/daughter _____.

Real Talk

When you ask a yes/no question (one that can be answered with *yes* or *no*), your voice rises at the end. *Do you have a birth certificate?*

But when a question begins with a wh-word (who, what, where, when, why, or how) your voice falls at the end. *What else do you need?*

Work with a partner. Ask some yes/no and wh-questions. Listen to each other to see which words you emphasize.

▪▪▪▪▪▪ Putting It Together

> **Wh-Questions**
>
> **Wh-questions begin with a question word, such as:**
>   *WHO   WHAT   WHERE   WHEN   WHY* or *HOW*
> To make a Wh-question, begin with the correct question word. The rest of the word order is the same as for yes/no questions.
>
> | | TO BE | MAIN VERB |
> |---|---|---|
>
> YES/NO Question: Is his name Hector? Does he live in Portland?
> WH-Question: **What** is his name? **Where** does he live?

Practice A

When Mrs. Feingold helps parents register their children for school, she has to ask them a lot of questions. Look at Mrs. Gonzalez's answers, and write the question Mrs. Feingold asked. Choose the appropriate question word.

1. _____?
   My son's name is Hector Gonzalez.

2. _____?
   G-O-N-Z-A-L-E-Z

3. _____?
   He's eight years old.

4. _____?
   He was born on May 23, 1983.

5. _____?
   Our address is 2365 Cranston Street.

6. _____?
   It's 555-3687.

7. _____?
   I work at Saint Joseph's Hospital.

8. _____?
   In case of an emergency, call me.

Practice B

Work with a partner. Write some wh-questions to interview each other. Ask your partner the questions. Then introduce each other to the class.

■■■■■ Read and Think

Read the chart, and try to guess the meanings of the underlined words.
Describe each level of school in your own words. Then answer the questions.

The American Public School System		
Entry Age	**School**	**Description**
5 yrs.	<u>Kindergarten</u>	In some school districts, children attend kindergarten for about three hours in the morning or afternoon. In other districts, children attend kindergarten all day.
6 yrs.	Elementary School 1st-5th grades	Children learn how to read, write, and do <u>basic</u> <u>math</u>. Students usually have one teacher who teaches them reading, math, science, and social studies. Sometimes there are special teachers for art, music, and P.E. (physical education).
11 yrs.	Junior High School* 6th-8th grades	Students at junior high schools have many teachers, one for each subject. They also have a <u>homeroom</u> teacher who looks after them.
14 yrs.	High School 9th-12th grades	Students take classes to get ready for <u>careers</u> or college. Students who plan to work right after high school take more <u>vocational</u> courses. They take typing, auto shop, or other classes that teach them job skills. Students who plan to go to college take more math, science, social studies, and English classes.

* Some school districts have middle schools instead of junior high schools.

1. Mr. and Mrs. Morris have four children: Judy is fifteen, Tom is twelve, David is eight, and Melissa is five. What grade is each child probably in? What kind of school does each child go to? Use the chart. How do you think the children get to school every morning?
2. Judy and David had bad report cards. They got bad marks in science, math, and social studies. Mr. and Mrs. Morris want to talk with their teachers. How many teachers will they have to talk to? Why?

In Your Community

Form groups by the communities in which you live to answer questions 1 and 2.

1. What schools do the children in your families attend?
2. Make a chart listing all of the elementary, junior high (or middle), and high schools in your neighborhood. Look in the yellow pages of your phone book under "Schools."
3. Make a chart showing the types of schools that children of different ages attend in your native countries. Compare the charts.

■■■■■ Figuring Out the U.S.

As you read the letter, circle the words you don't understand and try to guess their meanings.

A Letter to a Friend

Jean-Paul and Lakota are pen pals. They are friends who live far apart. They write letters to each other. In this letter, Jean-Paul wrote about his teacher.

Oct. 5
Dear Lakota,

I am very happy in school this year. My teacher is terrific! His name is Mr. Koutz. He's very friendly, and he tells a lot of jokes. Sometimes he sits on top of the desk when he teaches us!

Mr. Koutz asks us hard questions. We have to go to the library to find the answers in library books. Sometimes when we ask him a question, he says, "I don't know the answer. How can we find out?"

I've learned a lot in the first three weeks of school. We're studying about the ocean. We saw a movie about the explorers from Europe who crossed the Atlantic Ocean to America. We are building model boats. We have to read the directions and measure the wood. Next month we'll visit the aquarium to study the fish there. We'll draw pictures and write reports about the field trip.

Mr. Koutz is fun, but he makes the kids behave. If they don't do their work, he makes them stay after school. If they're really bad, they can't go on the field trips.

How is your teacher? Write soon.

Your friend,

Jean-Paul

Your Turn

Discuss the questions.

1. What does Mr. Koutz do that surprises you?
2. Are all American teachers like Mr. Koutz?
3. Would you like Mr. Koutz to teach the children in your family? Why? or why not?
4. How does Mr. Koutz make the students in his class behave?
5. How do teachers in your native country make children behave?
6. Compare teachers in this country with teachers in your native country.
7. Describe your favorite teachers from your native country.

> *Choose one of the questions and write about it.*

6 You Speak English at Home?

Before You Listen

1. Where are these people?
2. What do they need to take books out?
3. How long can they keep the books?
4. Is there a public library in your neighborhood?
5. What do you think Mrs. Feingold and Mrs. Diaz are talking about?

■■■■■ You Speak English at Home?

Listen carefully to the dialogue.

Mrs. Feingold: Congratulations, Mrs. Diaz! I saw your daughter's name on the honor roll list.

Mrs. Diaz: Thank you. I'm proud of her. I think speaking English at home has helped my children a lot.

Mrs. Feingold: You speak English at home? We don't.

Mrs. Diaz: What language do you speak?

Mrs. Feingold: We speak Russian, and our children are on the honor roll too. We don't want them to lose their native language.

Mrs. Diaz: I know how you feel.

Mrs. Feingold: When my father visits, he tells them stories in Russian.

Mrs. Diaz: That's great. Corazon used to speak a little Spanish. Now she doesn't even understand enough Spanish to talk to my mother.

Mrs. Feingold: That's too bad!

Mrs. Diaz: She's embarrassed to visit her cousins in Mexico. They tease her because she can't speak Spanish.

Mrs. Feingold: Oh, my! Well, they have bilingual programs at Corazon's school, and books here at the library, that would help her keep up her Spanish.

Words to Know

honor roll	tease	library
embarrassed	bilingual	
_____	_____	_____

Another Way to Say It

I'd rather .... I prefer to
great .... very nice
lose (a language) .... forget
keep up .... maintain

_____ .... _____

■■■■■ Talking It Over

Discuss the questions in pairs or groups.

1. Mrs. Feingold prefers to speak her native language at home. Look at the dialogue and find her reasons.
2. Mrs. Feingold doesn't want her children to "lose their native language." Why not?
3. Mrs. Diaz prefers to speak English at home. Look at the dialogue and find her reasons.
4. Corazon can't speak, read, or write Spanish. She doesn't understand her grandmother. How do you think her grandmother feels?
5. What language does your family speak at home? Do all of your family members prefer to speak the same language?
6. What are the advantages for children who can speak, read, and write more than one language? Make a list.
7. In the U.S., there are libraries in almost every town. It does not cost to borrow books. Are there many libraries in your native country? Who uses the libraries? Does it cost to borrow books?

Working Together

Work with a partner. One student plays the role of librarian. The other student asks the librarian for help getting a library card, finding books in another language, and borrowing a book.

Real Talk

Sometimes a yes/no question is asked in statement form.
  You speak English at home?
You can tell it is a question because:
• the voice rises at the end of the sentence, or
• it is written with a question mark.
This form is used mostly in informal conversation.

Used to

Used to expresses a situation that existed in the past but no longer exists.

Corazon **used to** speak a little Spanish. (She doesn't speak Spanish now.)

Use the simple form of the verb after *used to*.

Practice A

Make sentences with *used to*.

1. Mrs. Feingold lived in Russia. She doesn't live there anymore.
   <u>She used to live in Russia.</u>

2. Mrs. Feingold worked in a factory. She doesn't work in a factory anymore.
   _____

3. Mrs. Feingold was a machine operator. She isn't a machine operator now.
   _____

4. Mr. Feingold was an engineer.
   _____

5. Mr. and Mrs. Feingold dreamed about coming to the United States.
   _____

6. They studied English by listening to English language records.
   _____

7. Mr. and Mrs. Feingold thought that life was easy here.
   _____

Practice B

Work in a small group. Tell your own stories about life in your native countries and about coming to the United States. Use *used to*.

Example: *I used to think that everyone was rich in the U.S.*

■■■■■■ Read and Think

Read the interview and try to guess the meanings of the underlined words. Rephrase each paragraph. Then answer the questions below.

Three Kinds of English Programs

Interviewer: It is a <u>federal</u> law that schools must provide help with English and other subjects for students who don't speak English. How do you help these students in your school districts?

Dr. Laura Medina, Principal, Maplebrook Elementary School: We have many <u>LEP (Limited English Proficient)</u> students from Latin America. We want them to learn English and to do well in <u>mathematics</u>, <u>science</u>, and other subjects. We teach these subjects in Spanish so that the children will not fall behind the other children. Of course we teach them <u>ESL (English as a Second Language)</u> every day. They usually stay in the <u>bilingual program</u> about three years.

Mr. Fred McCarthy, Vice Principal, Lincoln Elementary School: We have children from 23 different countries who speak 12 different languages! We don't have a <u>bilingual program</u>. The children study math, science, and other subjects in English. We have one ESL classroom at each grade <u>level</u>, and each classroom has children who speak many different languages.

Mrs. Diane Santini, ESL Teacher: In my school district, we have very few **LEP** students. I teach **ESL** in the morning at the high school and in the afternoon at the elementary school. The students take their other classes with English-speaking students. I pull them out of their regular classes for the ESL class—this is called an <u>ESL Pullout Program</u>.

1. Which one of these three major ways of teaching English as a second language is often used if there are only a few LEP (Limited English Proficient) students in a school district?
2. Which one is best if there are many students with the same native language in the district?
3. Which one is best if there are many students from many language backgrounds in the district?

In Your Community

Work in small groups.

1. How many members of your group have children in school? How old are the children? Are they Limited English Proficient? What kinds of programs are they in? Bilingual, ESL, or all regular classes?
2. What are the advantages and disadvantages of these programs?

■■■■■ Figuring Out the U.S.

As you read the speech, circle the words you don't understand and try to guess their meanings.

A Success Story

James Hsu just graduated from Parkview High School. He was an excellent student and athlete there. Every year the Parents' Advisory Committee gives money to one student in the graduating class. This money is for

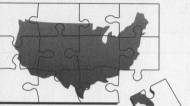

higher education. James won the scholarship this year. He is thanking the committee now.

I would like to thank the Parents' Advisory Committee for giving me money to go to college. I will be going to Stanford University.

When I came to the U.S., I was twelve years old. I went to school and was very scared because everybody spoke English. I spoke only Chinese. We were the first non-English-speaking family to come to this town.

My father found out about the Lau Decision in the United States. It is a law that says any student who doesn't speak English must be given some extra help. He told them about the law, and the school hired a special teacher to teach me English.

After one year of English as a Second Language instruction, I could speak English to other students and teachers. But I still had trouble studying science and social studies in English. The school gave me special help for four more years. The ESL teacher taught me how to study science, social studies, and other subjects in English.

After I graduate, I plan to help other immigrants and refugees who come to the U.S. I want to help them the way all of you helped me and my family.

Thank you very much.

Your Turn

Discuss the questions.

1. Is higher education expensive in your native country? Are there scholarships available? Who gives them?
2. James Hsu was scared when he first came here because he didn't speak or understand the language. Did you speak or understand much English when you first arrived? What things scared you?
3. What can you do if the children in your family are not getting help?

> *Choose one of the questions and write about it.*

Review Unit Two

Person A

All of the words in this puzzle are about education and the value of education. This is a cooperative crossword puzzle. Work with a partner to complete it. One of you is Person A, and the other is Person B. The sentences on your page will help you and your partner guess half of the missing words. Choose your answers from the words below. The sentences on your partner's page will help you and your partner guess the other half of the missing words. What is the hidden message?

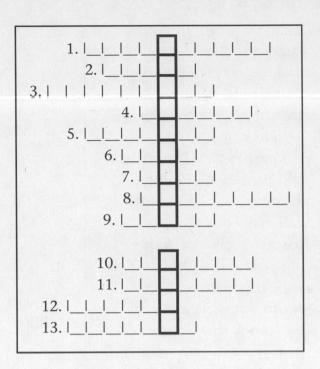

1. Mrs. Williams teaches third grade. She teaches at an _____ school.
3. A person who speaks two languages is _____ .
5. The Diaz and Feingold families love to read books. They often borrow books from the _____ .
7. Bernardo is in the eleventh grade. Bernardo goes to _____ school.
9. Mr. Williams is a banker. He knows how important education is. If you want to earn a lot of _____ , you need to get a good education.
11. Parents can help their children learn by _____ books to them.
13. In bilingual education programs, children spend time learning _____ as a second language.

money	English	grade	school
homework	diploma	family	library
reading	elementary	bilingual	high
math			

Person B

All of the words in this puzzle are about education and the value of education. This is a cooperative crossword puzzle. Work with a partner to complete it. One of you is Person A, and the other is Person B. The sentences on your page will help you and your partner guess half of the missing words. Choose your answers from the words below. The sentences on your partner's page will help you and your partner guess the other half of the missing words. What is the hidden message?

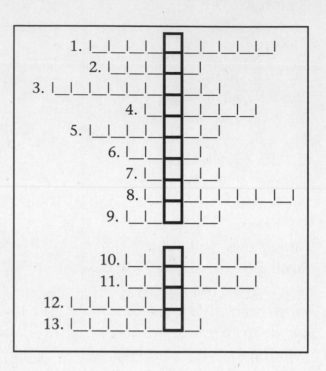

2. Corazon goes to high school. She is in the tenth _____.

4. Children must have proof of birth and immunization records to go to _____ .

6. The study of numbers in school is called _____ .

8. Every night I go home to study. I spend a couple of hours doing my _____ .

10. When you graduate from high school, you receive a high school _____ .

12. A mother and a father are the first people to teach a child. Education starts with the _____ .

money	English	grade	school
homework	diploma	family	library
reading	elementary	bilingual	high
math			

Before You Listen

1. Where are these people?
2. What do you think they are talking about?
3. What is the little boy thinking about his teacher?
4. What is Mrs. Williams thinking about her?
5. Why do you think they have different ideas about the same event?

■■■■■ She Patted Me on the Head

Mr. Chem: Hi, Mrs. Williams. How are you?

Mrs. Williams: Fine, thank you. Hi, Phon. How do you like your new teacher, Ms. Reilly?

Phon: OK, I guess.

Mr. Chem: She seems nice to me, but Phon doesn't act very happy. Last year he was much happier.

Mrs. Williams: What's the matter, Phon?

Phon: Ms. Reilly doesn't like me.

Mrs. Williams: I think she likes you very much. Last week she showed me the fantastic model airplane you made.

Phon: She didn't like it. She thought it was a dog's airplane.

Mr. Chem: A dog's airplane?

Phon: Yeah. She patted me on the head.

Mr. Chem: She patted you on the head? Oh, Mrs. Williams, that's very insulting to us.

Mrs. Williams: Oh, my goodness! I'm sure Ms. Reilly didn't know that. To US, that's how we show AFFECTION to a child.

Mr. Chem: Well, it's quite different for us.

Mrs. Williams: We need to learn about each other's customs. Maybe we should have a meeting with some of the other parents.

Words to Know

fantastic	patted	affection
model	insulting	customs
_____	_____	

Another Way to Say It

I guess .... I think
seems .... appears to be
What's the matter? .... What's wrong?
Oh, my goodness! .... Oh no!
_____ .... _____

■■■■■■ Talking It Over

Discuss the questions in pairs or groups.

1. What did Ms. Reilly do to upset Phon?
2. Why did it upset him? What did it mean to him?
3. Why did Ms. Reilly do it? What did it mean to her?
4. How do you show affection to a child in your native country?
5. Patting children on the head means one thing in the U.S. and something different in Cambodia. Are there other American customs that have a different meaning in your native country? What are they?
6. Are there customs in your native country that might seem strange to Americans? What are they?
7. Mrs. Williams wants Mr. Chem and some other parents to come to school for a meeting. She wants the parents and teachers to talk about customs. What customs from your native country should teachers know about? Make a list.
8. What American school customs should teachers explain to parents? Make a list.

Working Together

Work with a group of five or six people to finish this conversation. Imagine you are at the parent-teacher meeting to discuss customs. Use the lists from numbers 7 and 8 above to role-play the discussion among parents and teachers.

Mrs. Williams: I'm glad all of you could come tonight.
Mr. Chem: We are too. I think we can learn a lot from each other.

Real Talk

Sometimes certain words in a sentence are stressed (said louder or longer) to show a contrast or difference in meaning.

When talking about a custom that meant different things in different countries, Mr. Chem said:

That's very insulting to us.

Mrs. Williams said:

To US, that's how we show AFFECTION to a child.

Work with a partner. Take turns explaining a custom that means one thing in your native country and something else in the U.S. Use stress for contrast.

Talking about a Past Event

Use the past form of a verb to talk about a past event. All past forms of regular verbs end in *-ed*:

Last week Ms. Reilly show**ed** me the airplane.

Sometimes the last letter of the verb is doubled before adding *-ed*:

She pat**ted** me on the head.

Many common verbs are irregular. Because they are used every day, it is important to know them. See the Appendix for more verbs.

She **thought** it was a dog's airplane (think).

We **went** to a parent-teacher meeting last night (go).

Practice A

Answer the questions about the parent-teacher meeting last night.

Present	Past
begin	began
come	came
speak	spoke
take	took
tell	told
write	wrote

1. Did Mr. Chem tell his friends or his neighbors to come to the meeting?
   <u>He told his neighbors.</u>

2. Did the meeting begin at 7 or 8 P.M.?
   _____

3. Did many parents or a few parents come to the meeting?
   _____

4. Did they speak about student grades or different customs?
   _____

5. Did Ms. Reilly or Mrs. Williams take notes?
   _____

6. Did Mr. Chem or Mrs. Williams write a letter to the school newspaper?
   _____

Practice B

Write a short paragraph using the past tense about one of your customs that someone misunderstood.

■■■■■ Read and Think

Mrs. Tuy just received her daughter's report card. She doesn't understand it. She doesn't know if her daughter is doing well in school or if she is doing badly. Scan the report card to answer the questions.

Report Card

Jefferson Elementary School

__4__
Grade

Chanta Tuy
Student

Mr. Wayne Booker
Teacher

Ms. Maria Martinez
Principal

Grading Code:

A   Excellent
B   Very Good
C   Average
D   Below Average
F   Failing

Skill Code:

O   Outstanding
S   Satisfactory
N   Needs Improvement

Academic Subjects	1st	2nd	3rd
Math	A	B	
Reading	B	C	
Science	B	B–	
Social Studies	B	C+	

Behavior/ Social Growth

Listens well	S	N	
Shows effort	S	N	
Works independently	S	N	
Works well with others	S	N	

Comments: Chanta is having some problems this term.

Wayne Booker
Teacher's Signature

_____
Parent's Signature

Jefferson School
tel. 555-0580

1. Which grading period is this report card for?
2. The word *grade* has two different meanings in U.S. schools. It means both "year" and "mark" or "score."
   Chanta is nine years old. What grade is she in? What is her reading grade?
3. What grade did Chanta get in math?
4. What is Chanta's best grade? What is her worst grade?
5. What does **excellent** mean? **average**? **failing**?
6. Who is Mr. Booker? Who is Ms. Martinez?
7. Why is there a place for Mrs. Tuy to sign the report card?
8. Do you think that the comments on the report card are important?
9. Is there a big change in Chanta's performance at school?

In Your Community

How often are report cards sent out at your elementary school, junior high, and high school? Are they mailed home, sent home with the student, or given to the parents during the parent-teacher conference at school?

■■■■■ Figuring Out the U.S.

As you read the following announcements, circle the words you don't understand and try to guess their meanings.

Events Happening This Week at Jefferson School

Wednesday - 7:30 P.M. Back-to-School Night (Parent Orientation Night)—Come and meet your child's teacher. See your child's schoolwork and classroom. Find out about the exciting things your child is doing in school. Translators who speak Spanish, Japanese, and Khmer will be present. Refreshments will be served.

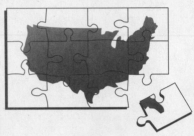

Thursday - 8:00 P.M. Parent Involvement Meeting—Dr. Belinda Costa will explain how parents can help their children study. She will talk about the difference between helping children and doing the work for them. Dr. Costa will also talk about the importance of good study habits. Translators who speak Spanish, Japanese, and Khmer will be present.

Friday - 6:00 P.M. International Potluck—To celebrate United Nations Children's Day, Jefferson School will hold an International Dinner. Please bring your favorite dish from your country. Multicultural entertainment will be provided by Jefferson students.

Room volunteers are needed—Room volunteers help with school parties, field trips, and other special classroom events. If you would like to be a room volunteer, please call Mrs. Feingold at 555-0580.

Bilingual aides are needed—Jefferson School wishes to hire several individuals to work as bilingual aides. Japanese, Khmer, or Spanish and a love of children are required. For information call Ms. Martinez at 555-0580.

Your Turn

Discuss the questions.

1. Have you been to a Back-to-School Night or to a Parent Meeting? Describe them. Do you have these in your native country?
2. What are good study habits? How can you help children learn good study habits?
3. What does everyone bring to a potluck dinner? Why do you think people have potluck dinners?
4. Do parents in your native country volunteer their time to help out at school? Do you think that this is a good idea? Why or why not?

> *Choose one of the questions and write about it.*

Fire! What Should We Do?

Before You Listen

1. Where are the children?
2. Who is taking care of them?
3. What is the girl wearing around her neck?
4. What just happened? How do you think it happened?
5. How could the children put the fire out? Should they try?

■■■■■■ Fire! What Should We Do?

Listen carefully to the dialogue.

Luddie: I'm hungry. Do we have to wait until Mom comes home?

Sasha: Well, there are some apples and bananas that Mom left for us.

Luddie: I don't want fruit. I want dinner.

Sasha: We should wait until Mom gets home. It's almost six. She'll be home soon.

Luddie: Let's surprise her. Let's make fried chicken. You know how to make it. You always help Mom. Come on, Sasha, please!

Sasha: I don't know . . . Maybe I should call Mom at the school. I'll see if she thinks we should cook.

Luddie: I thought you were the boss here. If you're so big, why do we have to ask her?

Sasha: Well, I guess it'll be all right. Mom is always so exhausted when she comes home. She'll be happy if dinner is ready.

Luddie: I'll help.

Sasha: The baby shouldn't be so close to the stove. We must be careful when we light the stove.

Luddie: Oh no, fire! What should we do?

Words to Know

surprise	boss	close
fried	exhausted	_____
_____	_____	

Another Way to Say It

have to	must
come on	please
be all right	be OK
_____	_____

1. Why are these children alone?
2. Where do you think their parents are?
3. What is the first thing that the children should do?
4. What else could the children do to put out the fire?
5. How could the fire have been avoided?
6. What should their parents tell them to avoid problems like this?
7. How old do you think these children are? How old do you think children should be before they are allowed to use the stove without an adult?
8. How old do you think children should be before they can be home on their own?
9. How do you think the children feel? How do you think the parents will feel?

Working Together

Work with your classmates and teacher to finish these conversations. Then practice with a partner.

Sasha is calling the fire department:

Fire Dept.: Fire Department. May I help you?
   Sasha: Hello! There's a fire in my kitchen!
Fire Dept.:
   Sasha:

Sasha is calling his mother:

Mrs. Feingold: Jefferson School. Mrs. Feingold speaking.
      Sasha: Mom! There's a fire in the kitchen!
Mrs. Feingold:
      Sasha:

Real Talk

Sometimes it's hard for someone to understand your name over the telephone. It helps to spell it and give a word as a reference for each letter. Listen as your teacher uses reference words to spell Sasha's last name.
   Feingold: *F* as in *flower*, *E* as in *east*, *I* as in *ice*.

Finish spelling Sasha's last name, using a common word as a reference for each letter. Then practice with a partner. Spell your family name and street name using reference words. Have your partner write them.

■ ■ ■ ■ ■ **Putting It Together**

Should/Shouldn't

Should means it's a good idea to do something.

Should not and its contracted form, *shouldn't*, mean it's not a good idea.

Use *should* and *shouldn't* with the main verb in a sentence to describe an action in the present or in the future.

    Example: You **should** be careful with fire.
                  Children **shouldn't** play with fire.

Practice A

The children are in danger! Give them some advice for right now. Then give their parents some advice for the future. Use *should* and *shouldn't*.

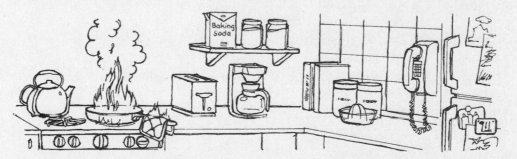

1. The children <u>should call 911.</u>
2. They _____
3. _____
4. Their parents <u>should tell them what to do in case of fire.</u>
5. They _____
6. They _____

Practice B

List some things your family *should* and *shouldn't* do to make your home and family safer.

    Example: *We should install a smoke detector.*

1. _____
2. _____
3. _____
4. _____
5. _____

Read the passage and try to guess the meanings of the underlined words.
Rephrase each paragraph.

In Case of Emergency

Fires, accidents, <u>poisoning</u>, and <u>severe</u> illness are all examples of
<u>emergencies</u>. In an emergency, you need to get help as soon as possible.
You need to telephone and ask for help.

In some areas, you can dial 911 to get emergency help. This is called
911 service. In these areas, you can dial 911 to get help from the fire
department, police department, or <u>ambulance</u>. In other areas, you may
need to dial the whole telephone number yourself. You can find out if you
have 911 service by looking in the front pages of your telephone directory.

In case of emergency, you also need to know the answers to questions
you may be asked. If you need an ambulance, the driver will ask you
where to go. If your child is sick, you may be asked for the age or <u>birth
date</u>. You may also be asked if your child has any <u>allergies</u>.

In Your Community

Use your telephone directory to fill in the chart below:

Emergency Telephone Numbers

Fire department _____
Police department _____
Ambulance _____
Hospital emergency room _____
Poison control center _____
Translator _____

Emergency Information

Your name _____

Your address _____

Your telephone number _____

Mom's work number _____ Dad's work number _____

Children's names and birth dates _____

_____

_____

Allergies _____

Doctor or clinic name and telephone number

_____

Pediatrician _____

■ ■ ■ ■ ■ Figuring Out the U.S.

As you read the passage, circle the words you don't understand and try to guess their meanings.

Child Safety Products

In the United States, there are many products that are made to keep young children safe and healthy.

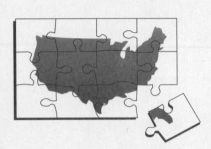

Child car safety seats—Each year thousands of children are killed in automobile accidents. Children who ride in safety seats in the back seats of cars are more protected from injury. Laws in the United States usually require children under four to sit in car seats when they ride in automobiles.

Childproof medicine bottles—Pills often look like candy to children. That's why most pill bottles have special childproof caps. All medicine should be stored out of reach of children.

Outlet covers—Curious children may try to put things in electric outlets. Stores sell plastic outlet covers to make it difficult for children to play with outlets. Many parents teach their children never to go near electric outlets.

Cabinet locks—Children often get into dangerous things such as cleaning supplies and tools, when their parents aren't looking. Cabinet locks prevent children from getting into these places where dangerous things are kept. Parents often teach their children not to touch dangerous things, such as tools, medicines, or cleaning supplies.

Your Turn

Discuss the questions.

1. In many states in the U.S., young children are required by law to ride in child car safety seats. Do you think that this is a good law?
2. Are all of these child safety products available in your native country?

Choose one of the questions and write about it.

9 I've Got Nothing Better to Do

Before You Listen

1. Where are these young people?
2. What are they doing?
3. Is this a good place for teenagers to spend time? Why or why not?

■■■■■■ I've Got Nothing Better to Do

Listen carefully to the dialogue.

Luis: Hey, man, leave me alone!

Bernardo: What are you doing in this place?

Luis: What does it look like I'm doing?

Bernardo: It looks like you're wasting your time and *my* money.

Luis: I've got nothing better to do.

Bernardo: You know Mom and Dad don't want you coming down here.

Luis: There's nothing wrong with this place. My friends are here.

Bernardo: Your friends are losers. You could get into a lot of trouble around here.

Luis: I'm not doing anything. I'm just hanging out and minding my own business.

Bernardo: You're throwing your life away.

Luis: Who cares? Life's a drag.

Bernardo: Stop feeling sorry for yourself. Get moving! I'm taking you home. Don't you have enough guts to try to make something of yourself?

Words to Know

place	losers	guts
wasting	feeling sorry for	_____
_____	_____	

Another Way to Say It

leave me alone .... don't bother me
hanging out .... passing time doing nothing
minding my own business .... not bothering anyone
Life's a drag. .... I'm unhappy with my life.
have enough guts .... be brave enough
make something of yourself .... improve your life

_____ .... _____

■ ■ ■ ■ ■ ■ Talking It Over

Discuss the questions in pairs or groups.

1. Where are Bernardo and Luis?
2. Bernardo is afraid that some of the people in the arcade are bad influences on Luis. Look at the picture on page 53. What bad things could happen to Luis in the arcade?
3. Why was Bernardo upset with Luis? Look at the dialogue again, and find his reasons.
4. Why did Luis want to stay at the arcade? Look at the dialogue again, and find his reason.
5. Do you think that Luis left the arcade with Bernardo? Why or why not?
6. What are some good ways that Luis could spend his time instead of going to the arcade?

Working Together

Bernardo and Luis have a younger brother, Arturo. Arturo wants to go to the arcade. Luis says it's a good place to go. Bernardo says it isn't. Work with your classmates and teacher to finish this conversation. Then practice with a partner.

Arturo: I want to go to the arcade because it'll be fun.
Bernardo: You shouldn't go to the arcade because the people there are bad influences.
Arturo:
Bernardo:

Real Talk

I'm just hangin' out and mindin' my own business.

When people speak English quickly, *hanging* sounds like *hangin'* and *minding* sounds like *mindin'*. Listen to your teacher say these sentences:

What are you doin' in this place?
I've got nothin' better to do.

Remember to write the full form—*doing,* for example.

■ ■ ■ ■ ■ Putting It Together

Reported Commands

When you report a command, use *told*, and change the command to the *to + verb* form. To report a negative command, use *not + to + verb*.

Arturo, come straight home from school.

Bernardo **told** me **to come** straight home from school.

Luis, don't hang around the arcade.

Bernardo **told** you **not to hang around** the arcade.

Practice A

What did they tell them to do? Answer with a reported command.

1. Get an after-school job.
   Don't waste your time.
   <u>My mother told me to get an after-school job.</u>
   <u>She told me not to waste my time.</u>

2. Go to the library after school.
   Don't waste your money at the shopping mall.
   _____
   _____

3. Do your homework after school.
   Don't hang out with those losers in the park.
   _____
   _____

Practice B

What did you tell your friend to do?

1. I told _____ to _____.

2. _____.

What did someone tell you not to do?

1. _____ told me not _____.

2. _____.

■■■■■ Read and Think

Read the passage and try to guess the meanings of the underlined words. Rephrase each paragraph. Then answer the questions.

After-School Programs for Teenagers

Many <u>organizations</u> plan after-school programs especially for <u>teenagers</u>. Several kinds of programs are offered by different groups. In this way, teens can choose an <u>activity</u> that interests them.

Junior highs and high schools provide a variety of after-school activities. Some examples are: intramural sports such as soccer and volleyball, <u>cheerleading</u>, and special-interest clubs, such as Spanish Club and Computer Club.

Other organizations that might offer programs for teens are: city park and <u>recreation</u> departments, the YMCA, the YWCA, and churches and <u>synagogues</u>. Here are some questions to ask when choosing a program for your teenager:

1. What is the purpose of the program?
   Some programs are designed to teach students a sport or skill. Other programs help young people do well in school.
2. Who participates in the activity?
   Some activities are only for girls or for boys. Other programs are <u>coeducational</u>. Also, check the required age.
3. What is the schedule?
   Some activities take place on weekends, some every day, and others only once or twice a week.
4. Are there any costs?
   Some activities are free, but there may be costs for <u>uniforms</u> or <u>supplies</u>.
5. Who supervises the program? How many adults are there for each teenager?
   Teenagers need to have good adult <u>role models</u>, people they can <u>respect</u> and <u>imitate</u>.

In Your Community

1. Form small groups by the communities in which you live. As a group, list some organizations that might have after-school programs for teenagers in your community.
2. Plan for each group member to call or visit one or more organizations.
3. Ask for their brochures about different after-school programs.
4. Make a group chart for your community with these headings:
   ORGANIZATION   ACTIVITY   AGE   BOYS/GIRLS   COST
5. Post it in your classroom.

■■■■■■ Figuring Out the U.S.

As you read the passage, circle the words you don't understand and try to guess their meanings.

Constructive After-School Activities

Laura Reyes is in the seventh grade. She was born in Puebla, Mexico, and lives in Texas now. Laura spends about ten to fifteen hours a week after school learning dances and songs for the Cinco de Mayo (May 5th)

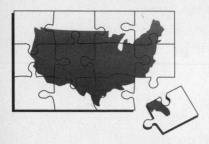

festival, a celebration in her Mexican-American community.

Antonio Mirano is in the tenth grade. He is from Italy. When he arrived in Los Angeles, he wanted to join a soccer team. He found out that his new school didn't have a team, so his father helped him start a soccer league. Antonio now plays soccer after school.

Patrick Lee is in the eighth grade. He came to Boston from Seoul, Korea. Even though Patrick doesn't speak much English, he eagerly does his homework. He studies English for many hours every day after school.

Marie Green is in the ninth grade. She is from a small village in Alaska. Now she lives in Chicago. Marie's mother taught her how to sew and make dress patterns. After school Marie works in a clothing factory. She helps make patterns in different sizes.

Your Turn

Discuss the questions.

1. Which after-school activity do you think is most enjoyable?
2. Which student do you think participates in the most constructive activity? Why do you think so?
3. What sports activities do teens enjoy in your native country? Are any of these sports played in your area in the U.S.? If yes, where and when are they played? If no, what would you need to do to organize a team for this sport?
4. What types of after-school jobs do young people have in your native country? Are any of these available in the U.S.?
5. Why do some students like to do homework? What can you do to encourage teenagers to do their homework?

> *Choose one of the questions and write about it.*

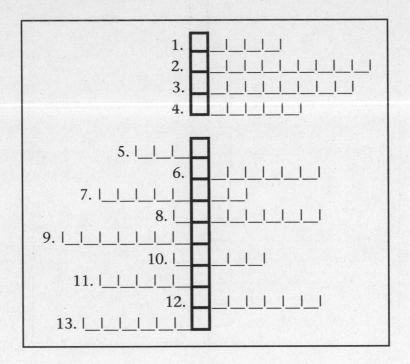

Person A

All of the words in this puzzle are about emergencies. This is a cooperative crossword puzzle. Work with a partner to complete it. One of you is Person A, and the other is Person B. The sentences on your page will help you and your partner guess half of the missing words. Choose your answers from the words below. The sentences on your partner's page will help you and your partner guess the other half of the missing words. What is the hidden message?

1. An old man just fell down in the street. He is holding his chest. I think he is having a _____ attack.
3. A person who saves people from swimming accidents is a _____ .
5. Smoke is coming out of the windows. I am calling to report a _____ .
7. A car just hit a utility pole. I'm calling to report an _____ .
9. Someone was hurt with a gun. I'm calling to report a _____ .
11. Please send an ambulance. My child drank some bleach that was under the sink. The label says it is _____ .
13. Someone broke into my apartment and stole a VCR and a television. I'm calling to report a _____ .

choking	fever	drowning	mugging	police
earthquake	heart	lifeguard	fire	accident
shooting	poison	robbery		

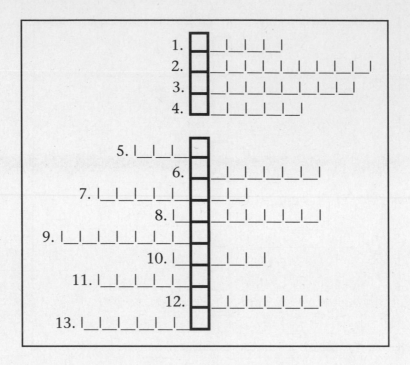

Person B

All of the words in this puzzle are about emergencies. This is a cooperative crossword puzzle. Work with a partner to complete it. One of you is Person A, and the other is Person B. The sentences on your page will help you and your partner guess half of the missing words. Choose your answers from the words below. The sentences on your partner's page will help you and your partner guess the other half of the missing words. What is the hidden message?

2. The ground is shaking. Oh no, it's an _____ .

4. Someone is screaming for help. Let's call the _____ .

6. Someone just knocked down a woman on the street and took her purse. I'm calling to report a _____ .

8. A swimmer is in trouble. Help! He's _____ .

10. My child feels very hot. His temperature is very high. It is 105°F (Fahrenheit). What should I do to bring down his _____ ?

12. A child has a lollipop stuck in his throat. He can't breathe. What should I do? The child is _____ .

choking	fever	drowning	mugging	police
earthquake	heart	lifeguard	fire	accident
shooting	poison	robbery		

Eat What's on Your Plate

Before You Listen

1. Who do you think these people are?
2. Where are they?
3. Why aren't there any women in the picture?
4. Do you think the boys like what they are eating? Why or why not?

■ ■ ■ ■ ■ ■ Eat What's on Your Plate

Listen carefully to the dialogue.

Mr. Feingold: Sasha, don't say that. That's not polite. Eat what's on your plate.

Mr. Calderon: If he won't eat that, there's some chicken and meatballs on the table.

Mr. Talofa: There are also cakes and pies that he could eat.

Mr. Feingold: He can't have dessert until he cleans his plate. When I was his age, we never had enough to eat.

Mr. Calderon: We didn't either. We ate what was set before us because there was nothing else.

Mr. Feingold: That's right!

Mr. Calderon: I'm just glad that we have plenty of food now. My boys can choose what they want to eat.

Mr. Talofa: My son knows he needs to eat everything on his plate.

Mr. Feingold: I try to teach Sasha that, but my wife lets him eat what he likes.

Mr. Talofa: My mother-in-law always cooks something special for my children.

Mr. Calderon: My wife's parents always cooked whatever the boys liked.

Mr. Feingold: Oh, grandparents!

Mr. Talofa: I guess it's their right to spoil their grandchildren.

Words To Know

annual banquet	choose	right
dessert	mother-in-law	spoil
_____	_____	_____

Another Way to Say It

That's not polite. .... That's rude.
cleans his plate .... eats all his food
set before us .... put on the table
plenty .... more than enough
choose .... select

_____ .... _____

▪▪▪▪▪▪ Talking It Over

Discuss the questions in pairs or groups.

1. Where are Mr. Feingold and Sasha? Why are they there?
2. Mr. Feingold thinks that Sasha should eat all of the food on his plate. Look at the dialogue and find his reasons.
3. Sasha doesn't want to eat the food on his plate. What do you think his reasons might be?
4. What does Mr. Talofa's mother-in-law do for his children?
5. Do you think that this upsets Mr. Talofa? Why or why not?
6. Mr. Calderon thinks that parents should let children choose what they want to eat. Do you agree with him?
7. Do parents in your native country sometimes have trouble making children eat? What do they do if this happens?
8. Do you think that children should eat everything on their plates?
9. Do you think that grandparents should spoil their grandchildren?

Working Together

Work with a partner to finish this conversation. Then practice it carefully.

Mr. Feingold: You should eat your food. You can't have any dessert until you finish.

    Sasha: I don't like this food. I don't even know what it is!

Mr. Feingold:

    Sasha:

Real Talk

Americans use the words *always* and *never* for emphasis.
    When I was his age, we *never* had enough to eat.
    My wife's parents *always* cooked whatever the boys liked.

It may not be exactly true that something *always* happened or *never* happened. However, it may seem that way to the speaker.

What did your parents *always* do when you were a child?

Make and Let

(**made**/forced) (**let**/permitted)

Sasha's father **made** him eat all of his food.
Then he **let** him have some cake.

Practice A

Mr. Wong is very strict. He thinks that children should always obey rules and listen to adults. Mrs. Wong is lenient. She thinks that children should be allowed to do whatever they want.

Choose *make* to enforce a rule or *let* to give permission.
(go to bed early)

Mr. Wong: I make the children go to bed early.

Mrs. Wong: I don't make the children go to bed early.

(stay up late)

Mrs. Wong: I let the children stay up late.

Mr. Wong: I don't let them stay up late.

1. (eat everything on their plates)

   Mrs. Wong: _____.

   Mr. Wong: _____.

2. (wash the dishes)

   Mrs. Wong: _____.

   Mr. Wong: _____.

3. (eat sweets)

   Mrs. Wong: _____.

   Mr. Wong: _____.

4. (watch TV)

   Mrs. Wong: _____.

   Mr. Wong: _____.

Practice B

Imagine that a baby-sitter is going to take care of your children. You are giving instructions. Use *let* and *make*.

Example: *Don't let them stay up until all hours.*

■■■■■ Read and Think

Read the passage and try to guess the meanings of the underlined words. Then answer the questions.

Special Education

Tanya Lee is not doing well in third grade. Her parents are worried. They have tried everything to make her do better. They have taken away underline privileges, such as watching TV and buying candy. They have promised her presents if she improves her grades. Sometimes Tanya tries very hard, but her grades don't get better. Finally, Tanya's teacher suggested a Special Education class. She arranged a meeting between Mrs. Lee and Mr. Berlin, the director of Special Education at Jefferson School.

Mrs. Lee:	What is the purpose of special education?
Mr. Berlin:	Special education is for students who have physical handicaps, learning disabilities, emotional problems, or who are blind or deaf.
Mrs. Lee:	What are learning disabilities?
Mr. Berlin:	Learning disabilities are special problems that some children have in learning. The child may be very intelligent, but she doesn't understand the way words are printed, or she may have trouble paying attention.
Mrs. Lee:	How do you decide if a child needs special help?
Mr. Berlin:	The child's teacher or parent can ask for the student to be tested.
Mrs. Lee:	What about children who are bilingual? How do you know if the child has special problems or if she just needs more time to learn English?
Mr. Berlin:	We always test students in their native language. We don't put children in Special Education programs just because they need more time to learn English.

1. How can a teacher decide if a student's poor grades are a result of a learning disability?
2. How can a teacher decide if a learning disability is a result of language problems?

In Your Community

Find out the information, and share it with your class.

1. Are there any special education classes at your local elementary school, junior high, or high school?
2. Who tests bilingual students in your community for placement in special education classes?

■ ■ ■ ■ ■ Figuring Out the U.S.

Here are some sayings that describe childhood and parenting in the U.S. They show that there are many different opinions about raising children in the United States. Match the saying on the left with the letter of the correct meaning on the right.

Sayings	Meanings
1. ___ Children should be seen and not heard.	A. Children have the right to feel loved, safe, and secure.
2. ___ It's too bad youth is wasted on the young.	B. If children want to do well in life, they should go to school.
3. ___ Education makes the man/woman.	C. Children should spend time having fun.
4. ___ All work and no play makes Jack a dull boy.	D. Children should be quiet when they are in public.
5. ___ Spare the rod and spoil the child.	E. Children don't know how good it is to be young.
6. ___ All children deserve a happy childhood.	F. Children must be spanked, or they will grow up to be selfish.

Your Turn

Discuss the questions.

1. Which sayings best describe how most people feel about youth and parenting in your native country?
2. Which sayings would most people in your native country disagree with?
3. Which saying best describes how you feel about youth and parenting?
4. Explain a saying about childhood or parenting from your native country.
5. Do you think parents should be strict or lenient? Why?

> **Choose one of the questions and write about it.**

11 Domestic Disturbance

Before You Listen

1. Who do you think these people are?
2. What do you think the police officers are thinking?
3. What do you think the woman and the boy in the apartment are thinking?
4. What do you think the man in the apartment is thinking?
5. What's wrong?

■■■■■■ Domestic Disturbance

Listen carefully to the dialogue.

Dispatcher: Domestic disturbance in progress, 1433 West Broadway.

Mavis: Oh no, not 1433 West Broadway!

Carlos: You've been there before?

Mavis: Several times.

Carlos: What's the story?

Mavis: Well, Phil is nice enough when he hasn't been drinking.

Carlos: But if he's had a few?

Mavis: If he's had a few drinks, he gets violent. Last month he beat up his wife, Sally. We had to take her to the hospital.

Carlos: Hmm . . . Are there any kids?

Mavis: Yes. Phil, Jr., is eight. Last time he tried to protect his mother, so his father hit him too. The child welfare department put Phil, Jr., in a foster home for awhile. But he's back at home now.

Carlos: Why doesn't she get a restraining order from the judge?

Mavis: Oh, the usual reasons. Sally says she still loves him.

Carlos: She loves him?

Mavis: Well, she thinks he will change. She is afraid that she won't be able to survive without him. She even feels that the attacks are her fault, although she's not responsible for them.

Words to Know

violent	foster home	survive
child welfare	restraining order	responsible
_____	_____	_____

Another Way to Say It

domestic disturbance .... family violence
in progress .... happening now
What's the story? .... What happened?
he's had a few .... he's been drinking alcohol
beat up .... hit several times

■■■■■ Talking It Over

Discuss the questions in pairs or groups.

1. Who do you think called the police? Do you think it was right to call the police? Why or why not?
2. Do you think the woman and child in the apartment are in danger? Why or why not?
3. What should the police do to help? Who else could help?
4. Why do you think Phil is angry?
5. What do you think are some of Phil's problems? Who could he go to for help?
6. What do you think are some of Sally's problems? Who could she go to for help?
7. Should Sally stay with Phil? Why or why not?
8. Should Phil be allowed to see Phil, Jr.? Why or why not?
9. Who could Phil, Jr., go to for help?
10. If Sally lived in your native country, who could help her? Who could help Phil and his son?

Working Together

This role play is for three people. Person A plays Phil, Jr., Person B plays Phil, and Person C plays Phyllis, Phil's sister.

Part I—Phil, Jr., tells his Aunt Phyllis that he is worried about his mom and dad. He thinks that his dad will hurt his mom. Aunt Phyllis thinks that it is terrible that her brother beats up his wife and son.

Part II—Phil and his sister are talking. Phil has not been drinking. Phyllis tells her brother that he has a problem. She tells him that she wants him to get help.

Real Talk

Hmm and *well* are used in conversation when the next speaker needs more time to answer a question or to think about what was just said.

Hmm . . . are there any kids?
Well, she thinks he will change.

Conditional Sentences

If I were Sally, I **would** go home to my parents.

If I were Sally, I **wouldn't** stay with him.

If I were Phil, Jr., I **would** be scared.

If I were Phil, I **wouldn't** drink anymore.

Practice A

Imagine that you are the people in the list below. Write sentences using this pattern.

			stay ...
	Phil		go ...
	Sally		leave ...
	Phil, Jr.		stop...
	Phil's mother		feel ...
If I were	Sally's brother	I would	be ...
	Phil's friend	I wouldn't	start ...
	Sally's friend		tell ...
	Carlos and Mavis		make ...

1. <u>If I were Phil, I would go to Alcoholics Anonymous.</u> _____

2. _____

3. _____

4. _____

5. _____

Practice B

Think of four relatives or friends. What would you do differently?

Example: *If I were my Uncle Theodore, I would learn English and get a*
           better job.

Read the passage and try to guess the meanings of the underlined words. Rephrase each paragraph. Then answer the questions.

Children's Rights

In the United States, children have many rights under the law. Adults are not allowed to <u>harm</u> children. Adults who were <u>abused</u> when they were children often have <u>emotional problems</u> when they become adults. <u>Child welfare authorities</u> can take children away from their parents if the children are neglected, endangered, or abused.

Here are three ways that adults sometimes harm children:

<u>Child neglect</u>—Neglect simply means that adults are not taking good care of their children. Some examples are: the child doesn't have warm clothes, or a small child is left alone without a <u>caretaker</u>.

<u>Child endangerment</u>—Children should be kept away from dangerous situations. A young child should never be near a hot stove. Children should not be in a car with a drunk driver. Children should not be left alone in cars.

<u>Child abuse</u>—This means that a child is hurt by an adult, <u>physically</u> or <u>emotionally</u>. A child should never be physically hurt by an adult. Some people believe that a child should never be <u>spanked</u>. Other people think that spanking a child teaches him or her to be good. Children suffer from emotional abuse when parents or other adults tell them that they are bad or stupid. <u>Sexual abuse</u> means that an adult engages in sexual activity with a child.

1. Who can take children away from their parents?
2. What are three ways an adult can harm a child?
3. Should parents spank their children? Why or why not?

In Your Community

Find out the information individually or in groups, and share it with your class.

1. Call the *Children and Family Services* numbers, usually listed in the telephone directory in the Government pages. Ask what happens if a child is abused by his or her parents. Compare this to what would happen for the same abuse in your native country. Share both with the class.
2. What are some reasons for taking children away from their parents in your community?
3. Is there a child abuse hot line in your community?
4. Are there "safe places" in your community where abused children can go for help?

■■■■■ Figuring Out the U.S.

As you read the passage, circle the words you don't understand and try to guess their meanings.

> Dear Mary,
>
> I am twenty-two years old. I have a three-year-old son and a two-year-old daughter. My husband divorced me a year and a half ago. The judge ordered him to pay me $500 a month to support our children. He hasn't paid the child support. Now I'm broke.
>
> I am very lonely because I have to stay home all day with two young children. Sometimes I just want to die, but I don't know what would happen to my children. What should I do?
>
> —Sad Suzanne in Sausalito

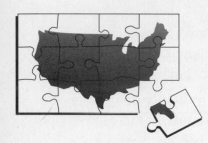

Believe it or not, this letter was written to a stranger. Suzanne (not her real name) doesn't know Mary. Mary writes an advice column for the newspaper. Suzanne's letter and Mary's answer will be printed in the newspaper.

A lot of Americans tell their problems to others. Some people ask family and friends for advice. Many ask strangers. Americans take their problems to a:

Minister, priest, or rabbi   Family services counselor

Legal Aid Society lawyer   Social Worker

Doctor, nurse   Women's crisis center counselor

Fortune-teller   Psychiatrist, psychotherapist

Your Turn

Discuss the questions.

1. Why do you think Suzanne is asking for advice from someone she doesn't know?
2. In your native country, do people talk about their problems, or do they think it is better to keep problems private? Do they talk to strangers? Do they talk to friends or family?
3. Imagine that Suzanne came to you to ask where to find help. Look at the list above. How would different people and agencies help her?
4. If you were Mary, what would you tell Suzanne?

> *Choose one of the questions and write about it.*

12 I Love Being a Doctor

Before You Listen

1. Who do you think these people are?
2. Where are they? How can you tell?
3. What is Mr. Fournier's job?
4. Why do you think the woman is there?

■■■■■ I Love Being a Doctor

Listen carefully to the dialogue.

Dr. Bashar: My name is Semra Bashar. I have a 2 P.M. appointment.

Mr. Fournier: Yes. I'm glad to meet you. What can I do for you?

Dr. Bashar: Well, I'd like some advice. In Turkey, I was a doctor, but I don't have an American medical license.

Mr. Fournier: Do you plan to practice medicine in the U.S.?

Dr. Bashar: Well, I'd like to, but I can't go to school all over again. I have a job in a factory right now.

Mr. Fournier: I understand. You love your profession, but you need to work right now.

Dr. Bashar: Yes. I love being a doctor, but I need to earn money to support my family.

Mr. Fournier: If you love working in medicine, there are a couple of things that I can recommend.

Dr. Bashar: Like what?

Mr. Fournier: There is an exam that you can take to get an American medical license. That can take months of study.

Dr. Bashar: Yes. I've heard of that. But . . .

Mr. Fournier: But you need to earn money soon. Well, we have programs that would train you as a nurse, a physical therapist, or a physician's assistant. With your background, you could complete one of those pretty quickly.

Dr. Bashar: But I need to earn money now. What should I do?

Words To Know

appointment	profession	nurse
license	recommend	physical therapist
factory	exam	background

Another Way to Say It

practice medicine .... work as a doctor
support my family .... earn enough money

Discuss the questions in pairs or groups.

1. Why can't Dr. Bashar work as a doctor in the U.S.?
2. Why did she go to see Mr. Fournier?
3. Do you think she should study to become a doctor in the U.S.? Why or why not?
4. Do you think she should become a nurse or a physical therapist? Why or why not?
5. Turkish is Dr. Bashar's first language. She feels more comfortable using Turkish than using English. Do you think that she should be allowed to take the exam to get an American medical license in Turkish? Why or why not?
6. In your native country, is it common for women to be doctors? Why or why not?

Working Together

It is difficult to get licenses and credentials to work as a teacher, lawyer, or doctor in the U.S. There are other jobs in education besides being a teacher. Examples are teacher's aide or school secretary.

Work with a small group. Choose one or more of these occupational fields: education, medicine, law, or a field of your choice. Using the help wanted ads of your newspaper for ideas, list all of the possible jobs in that field. Then put the jobs in order from the one that requires the *most* schooling to the one that requires the *least* amount of schooling.

Share your group's list with the entire class.

Real Talk

In informal conversation, Americans sometimes interrupt the speaker to finish a sentence. This is often seen as rude or a sign of impatience. However, it can be an attempt to show the speaker that the listener understands or sympathizes with the speaker.

Dr. Bashar: Yes. I've heard of that. But . . .
Mr. Fournier: *But* you need to earn money soon.

Describing People with *Who* Clauses

Who acts like the subject in a clause that describes.

Semra Bashar is a woman **who** wants to practice medicine.

Phil is a man **who** drinks too much.

Practice A

Go back through the chapters to complete these sentences about some of the people in the book. Write the chapter number first.

1. (Chapter 12) Mr. Fournier is a man <u>who tries to help students</u> .

2. (   ) Sally is a woman _____ .

3. (   ) Corazon is a girl _____ .

4. (   ) Bernardo is a boy _____ .

5. (   ) Mr. Williams _____ .

6. (   ) Mrs. Santos _____ .

7. (   ) Mrs. Feingold _____ .

8. (   ) Phon _____ .

Practice B

Now write sentences about people in your class.

Example: *Mr. Kim is a man who always has the right answer.*

1. _____

2. _____

3. _____

4. _____

■ ■ ■ ■ ■ **Read and Think**

Read the passage and circle the words you don't understand.

Higher Education

There are many different institutions of higher learning that students may attend after they receive a high school diploma. There are public community colleges, public and private colleges, and public and private universities. Public colleges and universities do not cost as much as private schools.

Community College	**College**	**University**
Community colleges offer degrees called Associate in Arts (A.A.) or Associate in Science (A.S.). It usually takes two years, going to school full time, to earn a degree. Some community colleges offer certificates for occupations such as Licensed Practical Nurse and Auto Mechanic.	Colleges offer degrees called Bachelor of Arts (B.A.) or Bachelor of Science (B.S.). It usually takes four years, going to school full time, to earn a degree. Some colleges also offer some advanced degrees. It takes at least one year after a Bachelor's degree to earn a Master of Arts (M.A.) or a Master of Science (M.S.) degree.	Universities offer Bachelor's, and Master's degrees. They also offer doctoral degrees (Ph.D.). It usually takes four to six years of study after a Bachelor's degree to earn a Ph.D.

In Your Community

Find out the information individually or in groups, and share it with your class.

1. Are there any community colleges, colleges, or universities in your community? What are they called? Are they public or private? Do they specialize in certain fields?
2. Obtain catalogues and brochures from the different colleges and universities in your area. What programs of study do they offer?
3. What public or private colleges or universities are there in your native country? Describe them.
4. Would you like to study at a college or university? What would you like to study?

As you read the passage, circle the words you don't understand and try to guess their meanings.

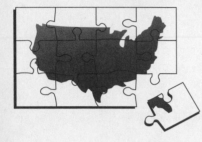

It's Never Too Late

I'm proud too. I'm buying a card for my wife. She's twenty-nine and just completed her High School Equivalency Examination (GED). She's going to start computer courses soon. Believe me, it's not easy going to school and studying when you have three small children.

I cook dinner on the nights she goes to school. The kids try to play quietly while she studies at home. Sometimes they take books and play "study like Mommy." When she finishes her computer course, she'll make good money as a computer operator. Two paychecks will make it possible for us to buy a house.

This card is for my husband. He's forty-five years old, and he just finished an electrician's course. He was a master electrician in our country, but he couldn't work here. The union said he needed to take courses to get his electrician's license. Now he has it! He can earn more money and get better jobs. Now people will know that he is a skilled craftsman.

Your Turn

Discuss the questions.

1. How old are the graduates we read about here? Do people in their 20s, 30s, 40s, and 50s go to school in your native country? Why or why not?
2. Look back at the comments. Why did these people go back to school? What benefits did they expect? What personal benefits are they experiencing?
3. What are the advantages and disadvantages for a child if his or her parent goes to school?
4. Do you know someone who has gone back to school and graduated? Tell about that person.
5. How do you feel about being in school? What are your plans after you finish this course?

Choose one of the questions and write about it.

Person A

In this book you have learned other ways to say the underlined words in the stories below. Work with your partner to find another way to say each underlined expression. Your partner has the list of expressions that go in your stories. You have the list of expressions that go in your partner's stories. Read your stories one at a time to your partner. Then read them again sentence by sentence. Work together to decide which expressions from your partner's list match the underlined expressions in your stories. Write the matching expressions from your partner's list on the lines on your page. Do not look at your partner's page.

The Banquet

We like going to our
club's <u>annual</u>[1] <u>banquet</u>[2].
We enjoy <u>being around</u>[3] lots of
people from our native country.
The conversations are <u>bilingual</u>[4].
We can <u>select</u>[5] American food
or food from our native country.
There is always <u>plenty</u>[6] to eat.
We stay up <u>until all hours</u>[7].

1. _____
2. _____
3. _____
4. _____
5. _____
6. _____
7. _____

Staying in School

Bernardo shouldn't <u>drop out
of</u>[8] school. His family works hard
to <u>make ends meet</u>[9]. If he <u>finishes</u>[10]
school, he'll be glad <u>in the
long run</u>[11].

8. _____
9. _____
10. _____
11. _____

A Good Movie

This is a good movie.
The man had a plane crash in the
mountains. He <u>had enough guts</u>[12]
to <u>survive</u>[13] alone for three years.
When his girlfriend came to
rescue him, he said, "Thanks, but
<u>I'd rather</u>[14] stay here."

12. _____
13. _____
14. _____

Expressions for Person B's Stories

concerned about	be OK	job without a future
expecting a baby	return	I am unhappy with my life.
worthless people	works as a doctor	pass the time doing nothing
Take it easy.	appear to be	ways of doing things
What's wrong?	Don't bother me.	

Person B

In this book, you have learned other ways to say the underlined words in the stories below. Work with your partner to find another way to say each underlined expression. Your partner has the list of expressions that go in your stories. You have the list of expressions that go in your partner's stories. Read your stories one at a time to your partner. Then read them again sentence by sentence. Work together to decide which expressions from your partner's list match the underlined expressions in your stories. Write the matching expressions from your partner's list on the lines on your page. Do not look at your partner's page.

Mrs. Santos Is Having a Baby

Mrs. Santos is pregnant[a]. She's worried about[b] having her baby in a new country. Her doctor says, "Don't worry[c]. Everything will be all right[d]."

a. _____
b. _____
c. _____
d. _____

"It's Not Too Late"

"What's the matter[e]? You seem[f] unhappy." "Leave me alone[g]. Life is a drag[h]. My friends are all losers[i]. We just hang out[j] all day long." "You can go back[k] to school. It's not too late to change."

e. _____
f. _____
g. _____
h. _____
i. _____
j. _____
k. _____

Dr. Bette

Bette is a young doctor. She practices medicine[l] all over the world. She has many interesting adventures. She travels to foreign countries and learns other people's customs[m]. She does not have a dead-end job[n]!

l. _____
m. _____
n. _____

Expressions for Person A's Stories

very late	choose	have enough money to live
fancy dinner	once a year	having contact with
in two languages	quit	was brave enough
more than enough	I prefer to	in the future
stay alive	completes	

Appendix

■■■■■ Community Resources for *Families and Schools*

Sometimes it's hard to know where to go or whom to call when you need help. In the U.S. there are many organizations to help with various situations and problems. Several are listed here. Sometimes a name is given because it is a national organization; others are simply kinds of organizations you may find in your community. Most of these will be listed in your telephone directory.

Chapter Topic	Organizations/ Resources	Description	Telephone Numbers in Your Community
1 Childbirth	Women, Infants, and Children (WIC)	U.S. government program of food aid	
	La Leche League	Breast-feeding	
	March of Dimes	Birth defects	
	Planned Parenthood	Birth control/health services	
	Clinics, hospitals, family services, women's health centers	Health care	
2 Child care	National Assoc. for the Education of Young Children	Child-care standards	
	National Child-Abuse Hotline	Child-abuse reporting	
	Daycare licensing agencies	Child-care standards	
	Child welfare agencies, churches/religious org.		
3 Children's tasks	School guidance departments	Counseling for children	
4 Dropping out of school	Libraries	Drop-out prevention programs	
	JTPA (Job Training and Partnership Act)	Job training with local businesses	
	Junior Achievement	Business projects	
	Upward Bound	Career counseling	
	Girls Club, Boys Club, after-school clubs		
5 U.S. schools	Board of Education		
6. Language	Library programs	Language classes	
	Ethnic community organizations	Ethnic activities	
	School foreign language/culture clubs	Teach language and give support	

Chapter	Topic	Organizations/Resources	Description	Telephone Numbers in Your Community
7	Family and school	PTA/PTO (Parent Teacher Assoc./Organization) Home-school coordinator Bilingual teachers/aides	Regular meetings for parents and teachers to work together	
8	Latchkey children	Libraries and religious organizations' after-school programs	Homework and entertainment activities	
		Emergency 911 Police, Fire departments	Emergency response	
		Poison Control Center	Identifies remedies for poisons	
9	After-school programs	YMCA/YWCA	Recreational activities	
		4-H	Farm/nature activities	
		Music groups Campfire Girls, Boy/Girl Scouts, Brownies, Cub Scouts	Outdoor education for children	
		Public library after-school programs	Help with homework	
10	Child-rearing practices	School social workers	Explain local customs	
		Health clinics	Help with safety and health hazards	
11	Family and the law	Legal Aid Society	Free legal services	
		Crisis hotlines	Emergency telephone services	
		Battered women's shelters	Temporary shelter for abused women	
		Victim assistance programs	Help for crime victims	
		Alcoholics Anonymous	Help for alcohol dependence	
		Al Anon	Help for families of alcoholics	
		Churches, other religious organizations	Help for all victims	
12	Adult and continuing education	Public schools	Adult night school is often held in high schools.	
		Community/junior colleges	Career education	
		Private/specialty schools	Commercial schools for secretaries, mechanics, legal assistants, hair stylists, computer operators. (Note: these careers require special licences to practice.)	

■■■■■ Irregular Verbs in *Families and Schools*

Basic Form	Simple Past	Past Participle
beat	beat	beaten
become	became	become
begin	began	begun
break	broke	broken
bring	brought	brought
build	built	built
buy	bought	bought
choose	chose	chosen
come	came	come
cost	cost	cost
do	did	done
draw	drew	drawn
drink	drank	drunk
eat	ate	eaten
fall	fell	fallen
feed	fed	fed
feel	felt	felt
find	found	found
forget	forgot	forgotten
get	got	gotten (or got)
give	gave	given
go	went	gone
hang	hung	hung
have	had	had
hear	heard	heard
hide	hid	hidden
hit	hit	hit
hold	held	held
keep	kept	kept
know	knew	known

Irregular Verbs in *Families and Schools* (continued)

Basic Form	Simple Past	Past Participle
leave	left	left
let	let	let
lose	lost	lost
make	made	made
mean	meant	meant
meet	met	met
pay	paid	paid
put	put	put
quit	quit	quit
read	read	read
ride	rode	ridden
rise	rose	risen
say	said	said
see	saw	seen
set	set	set
sing	sang	sung
speak	spoke	spoken
spend	spent	spent
strike	struck	struck
take	took	taken
teach	taught	taught
tell	told	told
think	thought	thought
throw	threw	thrown
understand	understood	understood
upset	upset	upset
wear	wore	worn
write	wrote	written

■■■■■ Index

*These words and phrases are found in the **Words to Know** and **Another Way to Say It** sections.*